A Critique of Moral Knowledge

A Critique of Moral Knowledge

by

YVES R. SIMON

Translated with an Introduction by
RALPH MCINERNY

Fordham University Press
New York
2002

© 2002 Copyright by FORDHAM UNIVERSITY PRESS.
All rights reserved.
LC 2002029478
ISBN 0-8232-2103-2 (*hardcover*)
ISBN 0-8232-2104-0 (*paperback*)

Library of Congress Cataloging-in Publication Data

Simon, Yves René Marie, 1903–1961.
   [Critique de la connaissance morale. English]
   A critique of moral knowledge / by Yves R. Simon ; translated with an introduction by Ralph McInerny.
     p. cm.
   Includes bibliographical references and index.
   ISBN 0-8232-2103-2—
ISBN 0-8232-2104-0 (pbk.)
   1. Christian ethics—Catholic authors.
2. Knowledge, Theory of.   I. Title.
BJ1249 .S4513   2002
170—dc21   2002029478

CONTENTS

Yves R. Simon as a Moral Philosopher   vii
  Ralph McInerny

1. The Concept of Practical Knowledge   1
2. Practical Wisdom   8
3. Intelligence, the Pupil of Love   17
4. The First Principles of the Practical Order   25
5. The Movement of Practical Thought   31
6. Moral Philosophy   41
7. Practically Practical Science   50
8. Christian Ethics   58
9. Moral Philosophy and the Science of Moral Acts   63
10. The Notion of Political Science: A Program   75

Bibliography   89

Index   93

YVES R. SIMON AS A MORAL PHILOSOPHER

The work of Yves R. Simon fascinates in many ways. There is first of all an encounter with a powerful mind, but it is ever the mind of a thinker whose feet are planted solidly on the ground. And this thinker thinks, not *ab ovo*, but within a tradition. Simon is a Thomist, and this in several ways. We find in his writings exegetical passages in which he turns his close attention to the text of Thomas and seeks to display its meaning. In this quest, he unself-consciously makes use of the great commentators. References to Cajetan and John of St. Thomas stud his work. In this he is like Jacques Maritain, and the similarity is by no means accidental. Simon is a grateful student who on crucial occasions rises to the defense of Maritain. First, then, Simon is a Thomist working in a tradition of interpretation that culminates in Maritain. But, second, he is all the more a Thomist in that, having assimilated that tradition, he carries it forward into hitherto uncharted territory.

The Jacques Maritain Center at the University of Notre Dame is the custodian of the papers of Yves Simon. The gift came in 144 folders that represented the topics or categories of the great encyclopedic task in which Simon was engaged when his life came to an end. We retained his categories as we transferred the papers to acid-free archival boxes, separating the pages with preserving sheets of paper. The material is now catalogued, computerized, and available for perusal.

I mention this in order to explain the diffidence I feel before the task I have been given here. Any student of Simon will be aware of the published books, including, of course, the growing list of posthumously published material. Impressive as the published output is, quantitatively it fades to insignificance in comparison with the unpublished material. Conscious of that, I am struck by the impertinence of discussing Simon as a moral philosopher in an introduction to his debut book. Our understanding of Simon has deepened with the subsequent works and will deepen further as scholars make greater use of the papers. I don't foresee any radical alteration in the interpretation of his thought but rather an enrichment of understanding. Even so, I think that too ambitious a summary statement is at present premature.

In what follows, I shall give a hint of what the reader can expect from Simon's discussion of degrees of practical knowledge and the notion of practical truth. I shall try to be both informative and inchoate, giving the reader a flavor of what awaits him, without abusing his palate.

Yves Simon's *Critique de la connaissance morale* was first published in 1934 and is thus celebrating its sixty-eighth birthday. And how better celebrate than by appearing at last in English? An English version of this book has long been wanted, and here finally it is. This work not only puts us at the dawn of Simon's career, but also is a fundamental contribution to moral philosophy. It starts at the beginning and goes on from there; and if it does not attempt to reach the end, we are struck by the clarity and order of the discussion. An understanding of this little book is essential for an orientation in Simon's work in moral and political philosophy.

Practical Knowledge

How to lay before his reader the notion of practical knowledge? Simon's discussion in his opening chapter is chiefly based on two texts, one from Aristotle, the other from Thomas Aquinas. Practical knowledge is distinguished from theoretical knowledge by Simon in the way set forth in the *locus classicus* in the *De anima* of Aristotle, III.10.433a13–18.

> Both of these then are capable of originating local movement, mind and appetite: (1) mind, that is, which calculates means to an end, i.e. mind practical (it differs from mind speculative in the character of its end); while (2) appetite is in every form of it relative to an end: for that which is the object of appetite is the stimulant of mind practical; and that which is last in the process of thinking is the beginning of the action.[1]

Every act of thinking is for the sake of an end, but when that end is simply truth, the thinking is called speculative. Practical thinking bears on an end which is *extra genus notitiae*, beyond thought; its end is not the perfecting of thinking as such, something brought

---

[1] *On the Soul* III.10.433a (*De Anima*, trans. J. A. Smith, in *The Works of Aristotle* III, ed. W. D. Ross [Oxford: Clarendon, 1931]).

about when truth is had, but the bringing into being of the thing thought. In the strong sense of speculative thinking, the objects are such that gaining the truth about them is the only possible end in view: they are not makable or doable by us. To think about coming downstairs or descending in an elevator, to say nothing of shaping an image of your mother-in-law with Play-Doh, is to think about what may be done or made. Yet there you are, supine in your Barcalounger, the picture of contemplation, thinking such thoughts. You might just as well be pondering the parallel postulate. Obviously, more distinctions are required.

Simon finds them in the *Summa theologiae*, Ia, q. 14, a. 16, where Thomas asks whether God has speculative knowledge of creatures. Thinking can be simply speculative or simply practical, or partly speculative and partly practical. In short, there are degrees of practical thinking. This is possible because there are several criteria in play—something Simon saw rising out of the text of Aristotle with which he began. Thomas gives three criteria:

> a science can be speculative in three ways. *First*, with respect to the things known, which are not subject to the knower's making or doing: the knowledge man has of natural and divine things is speculative in this way. *Second*, with respect to the way of knowing, as, for example, if a builder considers a house by defining it, distinguishing its kinds, and enumerating the universal traits any house must have. This is to consider something the knower could make but in a speculative manner, that is, not insofar as it is makable. It is makable when a form is applied to matter, not when it is analyzed into its universal formal prin-

ciples. *Third*, with respect to the end. [Here Thomas cites the *De anima* text quoted above.] Practical intellect is ordered to the end of operation, whereas the end of the speculative intellect is to consider the truth. So, if a builder should consider how a house might come into being but orders this knowledge not to the end of operation, but to knowing alone, his knowledge will be speculative with respect to its end, even though it deals with a makable thing.

In discussing the text in his first chapter, Simon relies on Cardinal Cajetan's commentary. That there are degrees of practical knowing is the clear meaning of the text. Completely practical knowledge is had when the thing known (or object), the way of knowing, and the end of the knower are all practical. But one can think about an operable object, and in a practical way—that is, think of the steps to be taken if the artifact is to be produced—yet not be engaged in the producing of it. And, of course, one can think of an operable object but in the same way one thinks about natural things, defining it, citing subtypes of it, etc.

The analysis of this passage from the *Summa* functions as the fundamental text to be explained and developed in the chapters that follow. But Simon turns in his second chapter to the discussion of prudence, whose act will provide an instance of completely practical knowledge. But he begins with an interesting remark: "Whatever the sense, or senses, of the phrase 'practical science' that we come to recognize, one thing is certain from the outset: it is not in practical science that the idea of practical knowledge is realized in all its purity" (no. 4).

Moral science will not exemplify what is meant by

completely practical knowledge. To define virtue and the species of virtues is to be thinking of things we can bring about or acquire by action, but this way of thinking of them is quite remote from such actions. Such knowledge can be called practical in only the minimal sense—its object is operable, but its mode and end are speculative. That kind of minimally practical knowledge shows up in moral science, but it is not perhaps characteristic of it. To think of operable objects in a manner that takes into account how they are brought about by our acts has been called virtually practical knowledge. Thinking of how justice might be served in certain circumstances is not as such an instance of the kind of just action being thought about by the moral philosopher.

Jacques Maritain, as is known, suggested four, not simply three, degrees of practical knowledge, and in chapter 7 Simon defends the proposed addition of *practically practical knowledge*.

Practical Truth

Completely practical knowledge is exemplified in singular actions. A singular act of prudence, or practical wisdom, counts as completely practical knowledge. In his discussion of prudence and its act, Simon is, of course, guided by Aristotle. Art and prudence are virtues of the practical intellect, the former being "identical with a state of capacity to make, involving a true course of reasoning" (NE VI.4.1140a20), the latter, "a reasoned and true state of capacity to act with regard to human goods" (1140b20). As a habit of intellect, prudence's truth might seem to present no difficulty. Isn't any thinking true when it puts together what is together in reality, and separates what is separate in reality? But that would make practical thinking indistinguishable from theoretical. Simon seeks further light from Aristotle.

> What affirmation and negation are in thinking, pursuit and avoidance are in desire; so that since moral virtue is a state of character concerned with choice, and choice is deliberate desire, therefore both the reasoning must be true and the desire right, if the choice is to be good, and the latter must pursue just what the former asserts. Now this kind of intellect and of truth is practical; of the intellect which is contemplative, not practical nor productive, the good and the bad state are truth and falsity respectively (for this is the work of everything intellectual); while of the part which is practical and intellectual the good state is truth in agreement with right desire [1139a21-22].[2]

Prudence, as a *virtue* of practical intellect, must ensure unfailing rectitude in the singular judgment of what I ought to do and sure guidance as director of appetite. But actions are singular, contingent occurrences in contingent settings. A virtuous habit of intellect must govern the attainment of the proper aim of intellectual judgment, that is, the true. But this, in turn, suggests necessity, not contingency. Simon works up this conflict, so that when he cites the text from the *Nicomachean Ethics*, which comes earlier than the definition of prudence he quoted, the Aris-

---

[2] The preceding three quotations from Aristotle are taken from *The Nichomachean Ethics*, trans. David Ross, rev. J. L. Ackrill and J. O. Urmson (Oxford: Oxford University Press, 1925), pp. 142, 143, and 138–39, respectively.

totelian text seems to provide the answer. But what kind of an answer is it?

To wheel in a new kind of truth might seem an *ad hoc* device to hurry past the difficulty. The demands of truth in the usual sense can obviously not be met. The mind's conformity with the contingent must be as fleeting as the corresponding fact. It is not that we cannot form and utter judgments about singular occurrences. "I am seated." "You are seated." "They are seated." "It's snowing outside." "The frost is on the pumpkin." "The needle reads 80." We do it all the time. There is a problem for two reasons. First, we are talking about a virtue that would ensure that the mind always makes true judgments, and, second, practical reason is not dedicated simply to the amassing of more or less accurate assessments of fleeting facts.

From the point of view of action, we seem advised to remain at a level of generality if we want certitude; such knowledge stands a chance of being unaffected by the kaleidoscope of contingency. Thus, natural law principles are distinguished from those less general guides and rules that express what by and large, *ut in pluribus*, is the way to act. Already at the level of generality, there is a falling away from certitude and necessity and a growing reflection of the contingency of the order of action that practical reason would direct. It seems to follow that, when the mind is engaged with the singular and contingent as such, truth must be so attenuated that it makes little sense to speak here of certainty and unerring direction on the part of reason. But that is just what prudence is taken to provide. The question becomes: Is this assurance had simply by changing the meaning of the key terms, so that what might seem to be reassuring is actually a linguistic shell game? "Of course, the judgment of prudence is certainly true! By 'true' and 'certain', however, I mean what elsewhere would be called false and unsure." Is that what is going on?

Simon cites St. Thomas's expression of the proposed distinction between speculative truth and practical truth.

> It should be said that the truth of practical intellect differs from that of speculative intellect, as is said in *Ethics* 6.2. The truth of speculative intellect consists of the intellect's conformity with reality. But since the intellect cannot be infallibly conformed with things in contingent matters, but only in necessary matters, no speculative habit of contingent things is an intellectual virtue, but only of necessary things. The truth of practical intellect consists in conformity with right appetite, a conformity which has no place in necessary matters which do not come about by the human will, but only in the contingent things that can come to be by us, whether internal doable things or external makable things. That is why the virtue of practical intellect is solely about contingent matters, art in the case of the makable, prudence in the case of the doable.[3]

Simon likes Cajetan's statement of the difficulty: "On the one hand, if prudence is an intellectual virtue, it must always express the true; but then it cannot have the contingent for its object, for contingency is the source of multiple errors. On the other hand, if prudence has the contingent for its object, it cannot

---

[3] *Summa theologiae*, IaIIae, q. 57, a. 5, ad 3; *Thomas Aquinas: Selected Writings*, ed. Ralph McInerny (Harmondsworth and New York: Penguin, 1998), p. 679.

always express the true, and then it is not an intellectual virtue" (no. 6). Clearly, if prudence is to be a sure deliverer of truth, a different conception of truth is required.

Speculative truth is had when the mind's judgment is in conformity with the way things are. Practical truth is had when the mind's judgment is in conformity with right appetite. The prudent man is sure that he is doing the right thing when he acts; his practical guiding judgment of the contingent circumstances in which he finds himself directs him unerringly to the good. Now, this sounds alarmingly like saying that our particular practical judgments are true if they serve our appetites. Simon takes up two questions at this point. The first has to do with what might be called the virtuous circle; the second, and more pressing, with the way false judgments about contingent facts are compatible with practical truth.

The practical judgment is said to be true when it is in conformity with *rectified* appetite, with a good will, not simply when it is at the service of any desire whatsoever. The latter would void 'true' of any meaning whatsoever, since then no practical judgment could fail to be true. If the practical judgment of prudence cannot fail to be true, this is because it is in conformity with *right* appetite. Aristotle suggested that pursuit and avoidance are appetitive analogues to affirmation and denial.

The Circle—Will is an intellectual appetite whose movement is informed by mind. Only the known good moves the will. Thus, if the will is rectified, this must be due to mind. If now we say that the mind's judgment is true when it is in conformity with rectified appetite, we seem to be moving in a circle. The mind's direction rectifies will's orientation, and the mind's judgment is rendered true because it is in conformity with rectified appetite. "To escape this apparent circle, it is sufficient to observe that the good direction of the will is understood with relation to the ends of the will, and that the prudential judgment concerns means" (no. 7). Prudence presupposes that will is ordered to the true good, that is, to the true end; its judgments bear on the way to achieve that end here and now, and its judgments will be true thanks to appetite's firm fix on the true good. Judgments about what that real good is are not subject to the same contingency as are those bearing on the here-and-now demands of the good in contingent circumstances.

Truth and Error—The arguments advanced against prudence's being a virtue capable of delivering certain and true judgments in the contingent order are meant to be answered by the concept of practical truth. But what generated those objections is not thereby altered.

Imagine a man who enters a building, finds lying on the floor an envelope addressed to another occupant, and slips it under the other's door. Alas, it is a letter bomb, and when the building rocks with the explosion, the good deed has had fatal results. In this little episode, we have by stipulation an agent whose character is such that he is inclined to do helpful things for others. Delivering the letter to the right address he judges to fall under the telos that guides his actions in such matters. He slips the envelope under the door, with disastrous results.

Such examples, which can easily be multiplied, are usually employed to illustrate involuntary action, as indeed they do. But let's look at it now from the angle of the problem Simon is discussing. Has the helpful tenant performed a good action? It was certainly no intention of his to blow up X, and one would have to be paranoid indeed to suspect every instance of the mail as being explosive. Implicit in his deed is the judgment that this envelope, addressed to X, contains some communication or other—a bill, a billet-doux, another breathtaking offer to purchase a platinum credit card—and so he acts. That is not the only judgment about the circumstances, but it is certainly one, and, in the event, a highly relevant one. And it is a false judgment. Does this vitiate his action?

If we took it to be the promise of prudence that we would never mistake our circumstances in this way, we would, of course, be sorely disappointed. But then of two things one. Either this is not the kind of judgment that is said always to be rendered true by its conformity with right will, or prudence sometimes fails, and then it is not a virtue.

Characteristically, Simon looks to the great commentators, and this time he cites John of St. Thomas—or Jean Poinsot, as John Deely would have us call him, which I shall be happy to do if he agrees to call St. Bonaventure Giovanni Fidanza.

> Take, for example, writes John of St. Thomas, a man in possession of wealth who doubts his entitlement to it. He does everything he can to ascertain the truth, without quelling his doubts. Very well, even though doubt persists concerning the truth of the matter, there is one point that is not doubtful: namely, that he has done what he could and should do. *There is certitude that the will is good,* and the judgment that regulates action in conformity with this good will is

infallible in its pure function of direction, not in its function of knowledge [no. 6].

This is still a fairly benign example. If such a man, having made the inquiries suggested and having acted on them, eventually finds that his claim is not grounded, what is the status of the acts he has performed up to this time?

They were based on what he now knows to be a false judgment of the validity of his claim. What we want to know is not simply whether a practical judgment may be made on the basis of fallible assessments of the facts, the deficiency being made up by the will's adherence to the true good, but whether false judgments of the facts vitiate the judgment of prudence.

Here I will suspend my discussion, in the hope of having whetted your desire to plunge into Yves Simon's enormously interesting interpretation of practical knowledge. To read Yves Simon is to be spurred on to undertaking the same questions and, while assimilating what he has said, push the inquiry along. That is what he did. That is what he invites us to do.

University of Notre Dame   RALPH MCINERNY

A Critique of Moral Knowledge

1
The Concept of Practical Knowledge

1. At the end of the treatise *On the Soul*, Aristotle asks what is the cause of our moving. He replies that it is both knowledge and desire, but immediately adds a clarification of the first term: the knowledge that causes movement is not just any sort of knowledge, it is practical knowledge.

> Both of these then are capable of originating local movement, mind and appetite: (1) mind, that is, which calculates means to an end, i.e. mind practical (it differs from mind speculative in the character of its end); while (2) appetite is in every form of it relative to an end: for that which is the object of appetite is the stimulant of mind practical; and that which is last in the process of thinking is the beginning of the action.[1]

---

[1] *On the Soul*, III.10.433a (*De Anima*, trans. J. A. Smith, in *The Works of Aristotle* III, ed. W. D. Ross [Oxford: Clarendon, 1931]). See also St. Thomas, *In III de anima*, lectio 15. Besides this passage from *On the Soul*, the most important Aristotelian texts concerning the general distinction of theoretical and practical intelligence seem to be: *De motu animalium*, VI.700b24, commented on by Albert the Great, *De motibus progressivis*, tractatus 1, chaps. 2, 3, and 4, and by Peter of Auvergne, *In de mot. an.*, lectiones 4–5 (a commentary included with those of St. Thomas on the *Parva Naturalia* in the Venice edition of 1566). For other texts of Aristotle on the same subject, see Georges Rodier, *Aristote: Traité de l'âme*, 2 vols. (Paris: Ernest Leroux, 1900), II, p. 537. For the texts

Let us try to disengage the reasons that make the idea of practical intellect come up like this in a theory of the causes of motion. Aristotle says that the knowledge directive of motion is not just any kind of knowledge but practical knowledge. Why not just any kind of knowledge? Because theoretical or speculative knowledge, knowledge pure and simple, belongs entirely to the order of specification or formal causality and is in itself entirely alien to the order of bringing something about. The object of speculative knowledge is a pure object, that is to say, purely a formal cause, purely a principle of what a thing is.[2] But the effective production of an act presupposes in the agent a twofold predetermination, existential as well as formal. Without a formal determination consisting of the *idea* of what is to be done, the act would never take place, since the agent would have no reason to act in one way as opposed to another; and without an existential predetermination—a *tendency* to act—the act would never exist, since the agent would have no reason to act or not act. In the world of things that lack knowledge, these determinations are one with their nature; but in human beings, tendency arises from knowledge. And this is how knowledge which reaches beyond its proper (pure) object to bring about its union with the object of desire becomes implicated in the practical order.

---

of St. Thomas, see Jacques Maritain, *The Degrees of Knowledge*, trans. Gerald B. Phelan (New York: Charles Scribner's Sons, 1959; repr. Notre Dame, Indiana: University of Notre Dame Press, 1995), Appendix VII, pp. 481–89.

[2] While every object, as such, is a formal or specifying cause, only the object of speculative knowledge is a pure object. In all other cases, the intelligibility of the object depends

Thus, the notion of practical knowledge stems from the need to account for the psychic regulation of an act with regard to its coming into being. Practical knowledge, like all knowledge, consists in the introduction of a formal cause within the soul, but it is a matter of a formal cause conjoined with a final cause, and it is this coming together of final and formal causality that determines its practical character. The proper principle of practical knowledge is not the object of knowledge (the true or formal cause), but the object of desire (the good or final cause); it follows that desire, which plays no intrinsic role in the constitution of theoretical knowledge, will play an essential role in the constitution of practical knowledge.

2. That is why in practical knowledge judgment enjoys an unconditional primacy. The first operation of the mind consists in the grasping of an essence and as such abstracts from existence,[3] whereas a judgment always expresses a relation to actual or possible existence. Is this a speculative judgment? The existence envisaged is stripped of any reference to final causality and remains in the realm of formal causality. Judgment, on the other hand, expressly involves existence and links knowledge of formal cause to final cause, the concretely existing object of desire. Practical knowledge does not abstract from existence, but only from individual cases, and all practical concepts imply a relation to existential effectuation, which can be ex-

---

on something other than its formal aspect. Thus, the object of desire is an end; the object of transitive action is an effect.

[3] At least to the degree that thought can abstract from existence; it can do so only imperfectly, because the essence remains a possibility of existence.

pressed only in judgment. Every practical concept depends on a judgment summoned by an end. One can define justice only if one has judged that to each should be rendered his due. So, we do not hesitate to say that, even though in knowledge pure and simple, and consequently in the total system of knowledge, the concept reigns supreme, in the order of practical knowledge the primacy belongs to judgment.[4]

3. We know that for St. Thomas theoretical intellect and practical intellect are not distinct faculties, but only distinct activities of the same faculty. "That which has only an accidental relation to the object of a faculty does not destroy the unity of the faculty . . . but it is accidental to the object grasped by intellect that it be related to action or not."[5] We must be careful lest this text, so easily misunderstood even without forcing the terms, be taken to destroy the notion of practical knowledge. It is accidental to the faculty of thought whether it be exercised with no other end than thought itself or with a view to action. We should understand this to mean simply that intelligence itself, *with respect to the express object of the faculty*, is unaffected by being related to action. We should not understand it to mean that there is no difference between the objects of speculative and practical thought, or that this difference is merely a consequence of a different *attitude* on the part of the thinking *subject*. For instance, a recent philosophical

---

[4] John of St. Thomas, *Logica*, I, Sum. 1, cap. 3, in *Cursus philosophicus thomisticus*, ed. Beatus Reiser, 3 vols. (Turin: Marietti, 1933), I, p. 10b15. In this chapter, which treats of the first operation of the mind, the author states that he will avoid any consideration of practical knowledge.

[5] *Summa theologiae, Ia,* q. 79, a. 11.

textbook, in a lengthy chapter on the classification of knowledge, in two lines dismisses, as lacking in objectivity, the Aristotelian division of sciences into theoretical, practical, and poetic.[6] But that is not how the better students of Aristotle have interpreted his distinction between speculative and practical knowledge. As they see it, this is an objective distinction precisely because it is imposed by the object. Thus, according to Cajetan, when we speak of objects of thought as related to action or not related to action, we are referring to something essential, not to something accidental. For the object of the practical intellect is that which *of itself and by its nature* must be dealt with by a faculty other than intelligence; the object of the speculative intellect is the true and is not of itself even tied to existence, let alone action. For instance, it is entirely accidental to the object of geometry that a person studying it may do so with an eye to earning money or procuring some honor.[7]

If the difference between the practical and the speculative sciences were only like the difference between the study of geometry pursued for itself and the study of geometry pursued for the purpose of graduating, their division would indeed have to be traced to a subjective point of view. But no one has ever maintained that geometry becomes a practical science when one studies it for a purpose distinct

---

[6] Émile Baudin, *Introduction générale à la philosophie* (Paris: J. de Gigord, 1921), p. 125.

[7] Cajetan, *In Iam*, q. 79, a. 2. John of St. Thomas, *Logica*, II, q. I, a. 4 (ed. Reiser, p. 269b18). See also John of St. Thomas, *Cursus theologicus*, I, disp. 2, a. 10, ed. Monks of Solesmes, 3 vols. (Paris: Desclée de Brouwer, 1931–1953), I, p. 395a.

from knowledge. Knowledge of the properties of geometric figures, regardless of circumstances, is theoretical knowledge and belongs to speculative science. By contrast, and regardless of distance from action, knowledge of the requirements of a righteous will is practical knowledge and belongs to practical science. Thus, even though it does not affect the faculty itself of intelligence, this is an objective division of knowledge based entirely on the difference between the objects to be attained.[8]

---

[8] Against the claim that there is a rigorous objective determination of the speculative or practical character of knowledge, one might be tempted to quote St. Thomas on the question of "Whether God has speculative knowledge of things?" *Summa theologiae*, Ia, q. 14, a. 16. But the main aim of this article seems to be to show that a speculative knowledge of creation is not wanting to God, even though divine knowledge is the *cause* of created things and invites comparison to that of the artist. *Summa theologiae*, Ia, q. 14, a. 8.

The entire text suggests the following schema:

1. A science whose object is not a matter for action (purely speculative).
2. A science whose object is a matter for action, but whose method and end remain speculative (relatively speculative and relatively practical).
3. A science whose object is a matter for action and whose method is practical but whose end remains speculative (relatively speculative and relatively practical).
4. A science whose object, method, and end are practical (absolutely practical).

But its point seems to be simply to raise the question of whether the practical or speculative character of a science can be decided purely by its object, since a science practical with respect to its object can be in other respects speculative.

Cajetan's commentary on this question helps us understand what it is all about. A science whose object is a matter for action but whose method and end remain speculative merits only accidentally to be called a practical science; thus, in a treatise on physics the chapter that studies the microscope belongs no more to practical science than any other chapter on optics. Indeed, when the physicist studies an optical or acoustical instrument that could only be a product of human art, what is practical is not the formal or specifying object of his study but rather the thing studied (*res scita*), a simple material object with no specifying role. There is no science whose (formal) object is practical and whose method is speculative.

Cajetan also notes that when a science is called speculative or practical because of its end, this can mean either the end of knowledge or the end of the knower. When the method of a science is practical, the end of the knower can remain speculative, but the end of the knowledge is necessarily practical. But it is clear enough that the end personally pursued by the knower in no wise alters the logical character of the science.

So it is that the four types of science distinguished by St. Thomas reduce to two:

1. A science whose formal object is simply an object of speculation (whether the material object, *res scita*, is or is not a matter for action is of no moment): *purely and simply speculative*.
2. A science practical by its formal object, by its method, and by its essential end (whatever may be the end pursued personally by the knower): *purely and simply practical*. It is the object that decides everything.

Notice, finally, that St. Thomas, when he speaks of a science practical in its object, but speculative in method and end, does not say *objectum*, but *res scita* (material object).

2
Practical Wisdom

4. Whatever the sense, or senses, of the phrase 'practical science' that we come to recognize, one thing is certain from the outset: it is not in practical science that the idea of practical knowledge is realized in all its purity. To be convinced of this, one need only consider that perfectly practical knowledge has to do with the singular. Nothing can be produced in existence except that which is wholly complete in the line of nature and provided with individuality. By contrast, the object of any science, including the practical, is to some degree a general object. Consequently, if one thinks a theory of practical knowledge should present it first in its fullest realization, the study of the virtues of art and prudence must precede the study of the practical sciences.[1]

---

[1] Because of the purpose of the present essay, we will concentrate almost exclusively on prudence. Texts that can be consulted on the subject of art are: Aristotle, *Nicomachean Ethics*, VI.4–5; St. Thomas, *In VI Ethic.*, lectiones 3–4; *Summa theologiae*, Ia, q. 117, a. 1; IaIIae, q. 57, aa. 3–4; IIaIIae, q. 47, a. 2, ad 3; *Summa contra gentiles*, II, 75, end; *In Boëthii de Trinitate*, q. 5, a. 1, ad 3; John of St. Thomas, *Logica*, Prologue (ed. Reiser, p. 5a 10); II, q. 1, a. 2 (ed. Reiser, pp. 256a36, 256b38, 258a17, 259a8); *Cursus theologicus*, IaIIae, disp. 16, in *Cursus theologicus in Summam theologicam d. Thomae*, 10 vols. (Paris: L. Vivès, 1883–1886), VI, p. 466b; Jacques Maritain, *Art and Scholasticism*, trans. Joseph W. Evans (New York: Charles Scribner's Sons, 1962), chap 4.

On prudence, see Aristotle, *Nicomachean Ethics*, VI.5. 1040a24, 1041a9ff.; St. Thomas, *In VI Ethic.*, lectiones 3–4,

5. Art is defined as the exact rational determination of things to be made, and prudence (or *practical wisdom*) as the exact rational determination of moral acts to be performed,[2] which leads us immediately into some most instructive difficulties. Since their function is to measure an action that ultimately depends on us, art and prudence clearly have the contingent for their objects. How, then, can we include "exact rational determination" in their definitions? Is there such a thing as rational determination of the contingent, of that which by definition can be otherwise than it is? Thus, there are many who do not think that our prudential acts can ever possess the unqualified certitude of rational determination. Yet look where such a denial leads. If there were no rational determination in prudence, the prudent man would be incapable of distinguishing between the false and the true. Or, to put it in another way, we would have to say, quite simply, that the human mind is made by nature to be defective in its practical function.[3]

7–9, 10–11; Summa theologiae, IaIIae, q. 57, aa. 4–6; q. 58, aa. 4–5; q. 65, a. 2; IaIIae, qq. 47–56; John of St. Thomas, *Cursus theologicus,* IaIIae, disp. 16, aa. 4–5 (ed. Vivès, VI, p. 466b); disp. 17, a. 2 (ed. Vivès, VI, p. 534a).

[2] Aristotle, *Nicomachean Ethics,* VI.4.1140a20; VI.5.1140b20; *Rhetoric,* I.9.1366b20. On prudence as wisdom, see St. Thomas, *Summa theologiae,* IIaIIae, q. 47, a. 2, ad 1.

[3] Here let us briefly distinguish prudence from art. Prudence as a virtue in the strict sense is a stable and good disposition that perfects the agent both from the point of view of the act to be done and from the point of view of the very exercise of that act. Since it is will, or, more generally, desire, that commands the exercise of the act, only habits that involve will or desire will be virtues in the strict sense. Art is not a disposition of that sort. For instance, we sometimes hear it said of an artist that he has talent, that he could paint great pictures, if he wanted to, but that he does not seem to care.

The response of Aristotle's school to this difficulty is well known: the truth of moral intelligence is not a speculative truth at all, but a practical truth. Whereas speculative truth consists in a relationship of conformity between judgment and reality, practical truth consists in a relationship of conformity of judgment with the movement of desire—if the movement of desire itself is as it ought to be.[4] There is conformity between judgment and the movement of desire when to the positive movement of desire with regard to a certain object (tendency, attraction, love) there corresponds in the mind, with regard to the same object, the act of affirmation, or to the negative movement of desire (repugnance, aversion, hate), an act of negation.[5]

> The truth of the practical intellect is understood otherwise than the truth of the speculative intellect. For one says that there is truth in the speculative intellect when the understanding is conformed with reality;

That could not happen to a virtuous man. For one who has, say, the virtue of justice is not merely capable of rendering to others their due in the sense that the lazy painter is capable of painting a masterpiece; the just man will actually do so every time the chance presents itself (if he is not prevented for accidental reasons). Thus, while art is a stable and good disposition that perfects its subject from the point of view of the act to be performed, prudence perfects the agent also from the point of view of the very exercise of the act which it presupposes, and this is a virtue in a stronger sense (*Summa theologiae, IaIIae,* q. 46, a. 3; q. 47, a. 1).

[4] *Nicomachean Ethics,* VI.2.1139a27. See St. Thomas's commentary on this passage, lectio 2; *IaIIae,* q. 57, a. 5, ad 3.

[5] *Nicomachean Ethics,* VI.2.1039a21. St. Thomas, *In VI Ethic.,* lectio 2. See also Franz Brentano, *The Origin of Our Knowledge of Right and Wrong,* trans. Roderick M. Chisholm and Elizabeth H. Schneewind, ed. Roderick M. Chisholm (New York: Humanities Press, 1969), p. 16.

and since intelligence cannot be infallibly conformed to the real in contingent matters, but only in necessary matters, it follows that no *habitus* having for its object the contingent is an intellectual virtue, and that there are virtues of the speculative intellect only with regard to the necessary. But the truth of the practical intellect is the conformity of intelligence with right desire, a conformity wholly out of place in necessary matters, which are not subject to the human will, but only with respect to contingent realities of which we can be the cause, whether these be interior moral acts, or the external results of the activity of fabricating.[6]

6. Is this practical truth, then, with respect to which intelligence, despite the contingency of the object, can enjoy perfect certitude, the unqualified truth of knowledge? Let us take the term 'knowledge' in its most rigorous sense. We know that in practical knowledge there is more than knowledge pure and simple, for practical knowledge includes also that which is designated by the term 'practical', whence arises the whole mystery that we tried to define metaphysically by speaking of a conjunction of final and formal cause. But now when we ask whether practical truth ensured by the virtues of art and prudence is the truth of knowledge, the question should be made precise, as follows: Is practical truth the truth of which the intentional formal cause, insofar as it is a formal cause, is capable?

The answer is not in doubt, for an affirmative reply would jeopardize the very definition of science. The primary notion of science from the point of view of

---

[6] *Summa theologiae,* IaIIae, q. 57, a. 5, ad 3.

the idea itself of knowledge is that of perfect knowledge. But if its object can be otherwise than it is, knowledge can never be perfect. Plato was right. There can be formal science only of the necessary.[7] Thus, practical truth, whose attainment is ensured by the virtues of art and prudence, can never be the truth of knowledge strictly speaking. And whoever maintains that it can has no way of distinguishing between theoretical science and the virtues of the practical intellect.

Cajetan poses with remarkable clarity the problem to which the notion of practical truth responds. On the one hand, if prudence is an intellectual virtue, it must always express the true; but then it cannot have the contingent for its object, for contingency is the source of multiple errors. On the other hand, if prudence has the contingent for its object, it cannot always express the true, and then it is not an intellectual virtue. This is a difficulty, he writes, from which one will not emerge so long as one insists that the perfection of the practical intellect consists in knowledge alone. Scotus, for instance, bases prudence exclusively on reason. For him prudence does not presuppose the goodness of desire, and if he speaks of a conformity between the right reason and the just will, this is to be taken in the sense that the act of will which, according to Scotus, follows the prudent judgment necessarily also conforms to it. But on this assumption mind would have to be capable of certitude in contingent matters, and that it cannot be. Therefore, either Scotist prudence is no virtue, or it

---

[7] *Posterior Analytics*, I.71b9; St. Thomas, *In I Post. Analyt.*, lectio 4.

has the necessary and universal, not the contingent, for its object. And if is the latter, one should speak no longer of prudence but of moral science. By contrast, for the disciple of Aristotle and St. Thomas the matter is clear. Since the perfection of knowledge is incompatible with the contingency of the object, perfection on the side of intelligence and contingency on the side of the object can coexist only if the perfection and truth involved concern not knowing but *some other act*. In fact, the perfection and truth of practical intelligence concern the act of *directing*, which is the proper act of practical intelligence, and this act of directing is infallibly true only if it conforms to the just will which precedes the prudential judgment.[8]

Thus, what is properly called true, when we say of practical knowledge that it is true practically, is not the formal cause introduced into the soul by knowledge, but *the pure relation of this formal cause to the final cause intended by the just will*. It remains possible that there could be error from the point of view of knowledge, speculative error; that the formal cause constituted by practical judgment could be inadequate to its object. But as long as this formal cause is in conformity with the inclination of a virtuous will, the prudent man will be assured that, with respect to the end pursued and all the circumstances, it is indeed this formal cause that ought to direct his actions and this practical judgment that he should embrace. Take, for example, writes John of St. Thomas, a man in possession of wealth who doubts his entitlement to it. He does everything he can to ascertain the truth,

---

[8] Cajetan, *In IamIIae*, q. 57, a. 5, ad 3. See also Réginald Garrigou-Lagrange, O.P., *Le réalisme du principe de finalité* (Paris: Desclée De Brouwer, 1932), p. 292.

without quelling his doubts. Very well, even though doubt persists concerning the truth of the matter, there is one point that is not doubtful: namely, that he has done what he could and should do. *There is certitude that the will is good*, and the judgment that regulates action in conformity with this good will is infallible in its pure function of direction, not in its function of knowledge.[9] Thus, when we speak of the

---

[9] John of St. Thomas, *Cursus theologicus*, IaIIae, disp. 16, a. 1. (ed. Vivès, VI, p. 437b). In summary, prudence being knowledge and practical knowledge, there is room in it for two truths, only one of which is essential and susceptible of certitude: a truth of knowledge, speculative truth, and a truth of guidance, practical truth. Besides the texts already cited, see *Summa theologiae*, IIaIIae, q. 47, a. 3, ad 2 ("Whether prudence knows singulars"). It is objected that the multitude of singular things is infinite; St. Thomas agrees that the infinity of singular things cannot be exhausted by human reason and that there results from this, for our prudence, an inevitable incertitude; but we check that incertitude by establishing experientially confirmed laws of frequency. Besides, at issue here is the truth of knowledge, speculative truth; the truth proper to the prudential judgment, the truth of guidance, is not affected by this imperfection.

It can happen that a prudential judgment has the fullness of practical truth while at the same time having only minimal speculative probability. Often circumstances oblige us to make a decision without giving us the time necessary to examine all aspects of the problem, to weigh the consequences of the side we are going to take, and to seek counsel from the wise. The fact that a decision can be perfectly true from a practical point of view while its speculative foundation is extremely weak should be clearly stated in any theory of prudence. An unintelligent, ignorant, and inexperienced man, without counsel, is capable, if his will is good, of making practically infallible decisions. But what must no less clearly be seen is the fact that in the prudential judgment speculative and practical truth tend naturally to coincide. The man whose will is good and who is resigned, when action demands it, to take a position on minimal speculative probabilities, is obliged, whenever possible, to inform himself better

truth of practical knowledge, it is necessary to put the accent strongly on the word *practical*.

7. Moreover, if the truth of practical knowledge consists in the conformity of judgment with a well-ordered will, we suppose, contrary to what Scotus supposes, that will is well ordered prior to practical judgment. But is it not the very function of prudence to ensure the good direction of the will, in such wise that a good will entails prudent judgment and pru-

---

on what should be done, and to seek as the basis of his decision a speculative probability as close to certitude as possible. The practical truth of the prudential judgment is independent of the results of the speculative inquiry that precedes it, but it is necessary that that inquiry be pursued with all our resources. Thus, a quite practical concern for honesty in decision gives rise to a research project from which the mind will derive great profit. An imbecile can possess the virtue of prudence and make practically true decisions that are speculatively ill-founded, but if his will is truly good, he will be drawn to a work of comparison and experience, to a docility toward better-endowed minds, which will soon make him cease being an imbecile.

[10] *In VI Ethic.*, lectio 2; *Summa theologiae*, IIaIIae, q. 47, a. 6 and Cajetan's commentary on it; John of St. Thomas, *Cursus theologicus*, disp. 16, a. 4 (ed. Vivès, VI, p. 468a). It remains to show what differences have to be preserved insofar as the definition of practical truth is applied to prudence in matters of human action, and to art, in the creation of things. Art, more intellectual than prudence, does not, like prudence, presuppose the goodness of will. That is why, in Aristotle's famous remark, it is better to sin against art on purpose than otherwise, whereas it is better to sin against prudence unwittingly than wittingly (*Nicomachean Ethics*, VI.5.1140b22). Nonetheless, St. Thomas expressly holds that the truth of practical intelligence, in the case of art as well as prudence, consists in conformity with a well-directed will. The reason is that the good direction of the will required for the certitude of judgment in art is understood with reference to the ends proper to art, whereas the good direction of the will required for the certitude of judgment in matters of prudence is understood with reference to the ends of human action. But of a

dent judgment entails a good will? To escape this apparent circle, it is sufficient to observe that the good direction of the will is understood with relation to the ends of the will, and that the prudential judgment concerns means. The virtue of prudence perfects only the act of voluntary choice; the tendency of will toward its end derives from the natural knowledge of the first principles of morality.[10]

---

man whose will is well ordered with respect to the ends of art or of any technique, we would say that he is a good worker, a good poet, or an able financier, not that he is a man of good will. Good will purely and simply is attributed only to someone whose will is good with respect to the ends of human action, someone who possesses a *morally* good will. For art as for prudence, a well-ordered will is necessary, but it is only when it is related to human ends that the good direction of the will suffices to make the will purely and simply good. See Cajetan, *In IamIIae*, q. 57, a. 5, ad 3; Maritain, *Art and Scholasticism*, chap. 4.

3
Intelligence, the Pupil of Love

8. The clearest example of affective knowledge is the practical judgment of prudence. In the order of scientific thought, judgment derives its justification from an anterior knowledge. But in the prudential decision the cause and justifying principle of judgment is the inclination of desire. *Intelligence here becomes the pupil of love.*[1] One who acts out of the instinct of virtue, knowing nothing of moral science, senses that it is repugnant to his nature to act otherwise, and this is sufficient for him.

Under what conditions will love be for intelligence a teacher worthy of confidence? The intrusion of the heart into matters of judgment customarily causes error, and that in the practical as well as in the theoretical order. Most men act by following their instincts and most men err. This is because a judgment decided by the inclination of the heart is true only when the heart itself is in accord with the object of the judgment, and if there exists sympathy and con-

---

[1] On knowledge through affective connaturality, see *Summa theologiae*, Ia, q. 1, a. 6, ad 3; IaIIae, q. 65, aa. 1–2; q. 95, a. 2, ad 4; IIaIIae, q. 45, a. 2; John of St. Thomas, *Cursus theologicus*, I–II, disp. 18, a. 4 (ed. Vivès, VI, pp. 634ff.); Jacques Maritain, *Réflexions sur l'intelligence et sur sa vie propre* (Paris: Nouvelle Librairie Nationale, 1924), pp. 88, 110ff.; Max Scheler, *The Nature of Sympathy*, trans. Peter Heath, ed. Werner Stark (New Haven, Connecticut: Yale University Press, 1954).

sonance between the object to which the judgment relates and the desire that decides the judgment.

There is sympathy between two persons when they are disposed to have the same feelings when confronted by the same stimulus. We extend to a bereaved family our sympathy; that is to say, the event that saddens them causes sadness in us as well. There is sympathy between desire and the object of judgment when the passions of desire correspond to the passions of the object, in such a way that to the objective demand of an affirmative judgment, desire reacts with a positive tendency, and to the objective demand of a judgment of negation, with repugnance. But for this sympathy to exist, desire must in some way have *become* the object of which intelligence must judge in conformity with the movements of desire.[2]

The virtuous man, in order to judge well what concerns virtue, can do no better than follow the inclination of his heart. This is because virtue is established in him as an active force; the regulative law of his desire is the very law of the virtue.[3] Equally, a soul

---

[2] "Amor transit in conditionem objecti." John of St. Thomas, *Cursus theologicus, IaIIae*, disp. 18, a. 4 (ed. Vivès, VI, p. 638).

[3] *Nicomachean Ethics*, X.5.1176a17. For Aristotle it is so essential that the concrete rule of virtue be arrived at by the affective judgment of the wise man that his definition of virtue includes specific reference to such a judgment. See ibid., VI.6.1106b36.

The characteristics of practical wisdom are wonderfully summed up in this quatrain by Charles Maurras (from *La musique intérieure* [Paris: B. Grasset, 1925]):

> *Si votre coeur est humble et votre âme très pure,*
> *Venez, il est permis de le dire tout bas,*
> *De toutes les grandeurs vous êtes la mesure,*
> *Un ciel intérieure illumine vos pas.*

divinized by the intimate presence of God takes no risk in judging divine things according to its own inclinations, for God Himself, present in it, incites and measures the movement of its love. Or, to put it in another way, the certitude of affective knowledge requires the establishment of the object to be known in the heart of the knowing subject. Whenever the object to be known has not been so introduced within us as to regulate the movements of our desire in the way the constitutive form of a nature regulates the tendencies deriving from that nature, the docility of judgment to the inclination of the heart will run the risk of being a source of delusion.

This is why it is important to distinguish with the utmost care knowledge by intellectual connaturality, whose contribution in establishing speculative truth is by no means negligible, and knowledge *by affective connaturality*, which plays its proper role in practical thought and in mystical experience.[4] It often happens

---

The first line indicates the proper condition of practical wisdom, complete honesty of heart; the second line recalls that it is discreet and surrounds itself with silence: the wisdom of the prudent man, having value chiefly for the prudent man himself and remaining, with respect to what is best in it, incommunicable, does not demand to be expressed in words as science does; in the third line we recognize the formula of Aristotle which itself transposes the celebrated remark of Protagoras from the speculative order, where it is false, to the practical where, guarding all proportions, it is true; finally, the last line assigns, *first*, the source of the prudential light, which comes not directly from the object but from the interior of the soul, and, *second*, the function of this light: to illumine *our steps*, our conduct, our action.

[4] In saying that affective knowledge, in the natural order, seems to have for its proper object things to be done, we do not mean to restrict its role to the prudential direction of our actions. To be sure, it is when it is a matter of an act to be

that, prior to any demonstration, a scholar sees flashing before him wrapped in peculiar familiarity the answer that he was looking for and of which he is now completely certain. Still unable formally to justify what he sees, that is, to attach this new truth to those previously acquired, our scholar is apt to speak of intuition and to admit that he owes his discovery not to his mind but to his heart.[5] But he is mistaken, for

---

performed or of a value to be existentially realized that the conditions for the perfect functioning of affective knowledge are to be found; doubtless, the supernatural order exempted, it is only then that it is absolutely necessary and capable of absolute certitude.

It seems, however, that it can have a role to play any time that it is a matter of grasping values, not only those to be realized by our liberty, but also values realized in things independent of our liberty. Individual knowledge of persons, history, sociology, even psychology to the degree that it extends to existential realizations (something it does more and more nowadays), appears to require acts of affective knowledge whose function moreover can be *heuristic* and strictly subject to the control of rational knowledge. Abundant indications on this topic are found in the work, uneven but profound, of Max Scheler.

An inquiry into the psychology of discovery would no doubt show that even in speculative matters affective knowledge can exercise a heuristic role of undeniable fecundity, and that it becomes a source of illusions only when it goes beyond this heuristic role and attempts to supplant rational demonstration. On this subject, Buytendijk's report on the differences between human and animal behavior can be profitably pondered (*Vues sur la psychologie animale*, Cahiers de philosophie de la nature 4 [Paris: Vrin, 1930]). On knowledge by intellectual connaturality, see Maritain, *Réflexions sur l'intelligence*, pp. 112–13.

[5] See Pierre Boutroux, *Les mathematiques* (Paris: Albin Michel, 1922), p. 65: "It appears that the first Pythagoreans considered mathematical truths to be secret treasures that should not be profaned by passing the means of acquiring them on to just anyone who happened along. Nor did they take the

the heart he listens to is only *the heart of his mind*. The inclination he follows is the natural tendency of the mind toward the true, which is the object of intelligence and its good. In his discussion of the first cosmological systems, Aristotle observes that his predecessors were not mistaken in holding that the principles of physical things are contraries, even though they lacked formal arguments to establish their thesis. How did they know? Because, as St. Thomas comments, the truth had in some way constrained them. "The true is, in fact, the good of the intelligence; it is the good to which intelligence is naturally related. Thus, just as things deprived of intelligence are borne toward their ends without perceiving the reason for their activity, so *sometimes* human intelligence is carried to the truth as the result of natural inclination without grasping the reason for what it affirms."[6] Here St. Thomas is thinking of a happy outcome due to the natural instinct that sometimes leads even minds stuck in error to the true. But

---

trouble to codify and formulate the methods that permit any ordinary person to learn the properties of numbers and figures. What was important to them was to know that these properties exist. And this they knew even perhaps before finding absolutely probative arguments for them. There are, in fact, cases where the moral conviction that we can possess truth without formal proof has, in the circumstances, the value of a certainty. In such cases, this conviction, though it does not exist for a critical or skeptical mind, suffices nonetheless to excite the true scientist, who has the sharpest sense of speculative truth." *Moral conviction*: an improper phrase but one most suggestive in its very impropriety. The heart has nothing to do with the convictions of mathematicians, but the certitude resulting from intellectual connaturality, prior to demonstration, resembles in its immediacy and familiarity the certitude resulting from affective connaturality.

[6] *In I Physics.*, lectio 10.

for this to occur regularly, that is, for intellectual connaturality to sustain such intuition in all stages of our thought, the mind's affinity with the true must be reinforced by a kind of second nature, which is nothing else than the scientific *habitus*.

Henri Bergson, in unforgettable pages, has celebrated the vivifying and unifying intuition whose presence he rightly recognizes at the source of every great philosophy. As he describes it, it is confused knowledge, proceeding, above all, *by way of negation*.

> It seems to me that intuition often functions in speculative matters like Socrates' demon in practical life; in any case, it is in this form that it begins and in this form, too, that it continues to provide its clearest manifestations: it forbids. Before received opinions, theses that appear evident, affirmations that have up until now passed for scientific, it breathes in the ear of the philosopher the word *impossible*. . . . Impossible, even when facts and arguments invite you to think it possible, real, certain. Impossible, because a certain experience, confused perhaps but decisive, speaks to you with a secret voice, that it is incompatible with the facts cited and the arguments given, that these facts have been badly observed and these arguments are false. What a singular power this instinctive capacity for negation. . . . Why has it not gotten more attention from the historians of philosophy? Is it not clear that the first step of philosophy, when its thoughts were yet poorly based and there was nothing definitive in its teaching, was definitively to reject certain things? Later will come variations in what it affirms, but it does not vary in what it denies. And if it varies in what it affirms, this will still be due to

the power of negation immanent in intuition or in its image.[7]

In the case of the metaphysician, the mathematician, the physicist, this intuition comes chiefly from intellectual connaturality, or else it runs the risk of being an illusion. With the moralist, on the contrary, it seems that philosophical intuition ought to stem from affective connaturality. If one applied to a moralist like Proudhon the method of reduction that Bergson, in the work cited, applies to Berkeley, one would see that the essence of his thought, changeless through incessant revolutions, comes down to an extraordinarily vivid and passionate vision of the demands of commutative justice, a devouring intuition, strong enough to resist all arguments raised against it and superior in its certitude to all the demonstrations that will arise from it.[8] But it is clear that affective intuition, whether at the point of departure of moral philosophy or in its subsequent developments, will surely avoid illusion only if the moralist himself is a

---

[7] Henri Bergson, *L'intuition philosophique* (Paris: Armand Colin, 1911), pp. 19–21.

[8] Pierre-Joseph Proudhon, *Third Notebook* (unpublished): "Whence comes to me this passion for justice which controls me, irritates me, enrages me? . . . I cannot explain it to myself. It is my God, my religion, my all, and if I try to justify it by philosophical argument, I cannot do it.

"Why are not poets, authors, mystics as good as the scientist?

"It is my star that guides me against them.

"Am I right to ask anything of them? —*No*.

"I cannot be a spiritualist or a materialist, atheist or humanitarian, and when I have gotten rid of all these mysticisms, I find myself in the grips of a greater mysticism; justice is the mystery of mysteries."

virtuous person, the inclination of whose heart does not run the risk of being tugged in a direction away from good. The professor of morality who himself leads an immoral life is bound to have false intuitions, if he has any at all. Indeed, it would be better for the truth of his teaching if he had none. But how boring the discourse of a professor without intuitions!

4
The First Principles of the Practical Order

9. Having said that knowledge is a principle of motion and having made it clear that only practical knowledge is motivating, Aristotle goes on to say that there are two species of practical knowledge, the one having the universal for its object, the other the singular, and that the knowledge that moves is properly that which has the singular for its object.[1] If we should say, as Thomas suggests in his commentary, that both species of practical knowledge cause motion, universal practical knowledge moves in the manner of the first unmoved cause, whereas particular practical knowledge does so as a proximate cause in some way applied to motion. Thus, besides properly motivating knowledge, which is practical in the full sense of the term, there is another knowledge, also describable as practical because it is in some sense

---

[1] See *On the Soul*, III.11.434a16ff.: "The faculty of knowing is never moved but remains at rest. Since the one premiss or judgement is universal and the other deals with the particular (for the first tells us that such and such a kind of man should do such and such a kind of act, and the second that *this* is an act of the kind meant, and I a person of the type intended), it is the latter opinion that really originates movement, not the universal; or rather it is both, but the one does so while it remains in a state more like rest, while the other partakes in movement" (trans. J. A. Smith). See St. Thomas, *In III de anima*, lectio 16, nn. 845–46.

action-guiding and unites an object of desire and an object of thought, but not fully moving or practical because it remains universal. But the division of knowledge into speculative and practical being exhaustive, whatever is deficient in the practical will be classified as speculation. Thus, to the degree that it is imperfectly practical, knowledge is speculative, and imperfectly practical knowledge can therefore be called *speculative-practical* knowledge (or universal practical knowledge).

10. When from this imperfectly practical knowledge, which, to whatever degree, remains linked to the universal, we pass to fully practical knowledge—call it *practico-practical knowledge*—which opens onto the singular, something absolutely new is introduced. Indeed, just as the singular is irreducible to the universal, practico-practical knowledge cannot be reduced to any other sort of knowledge. But as the distance between the universal and the singular admits of degrees, speculative-practical knowledge exhibits definite levels and approximates practico-practical knowledge in reverse proportion to its generality.

We can represent this by an upside-down cone whose tip touches a plane surface. The plane surface stands for the world of the individual. Only the tip of the cone, representing the prudential judgment, the practico-practical, is in contact with it; within the cone we can inscribe circles at different levels, such that their unequal area is in direct relation to their distance from the tip: these circles represent speculative-practical knowledge in its various degrees of generality.

This image captures perfectly the two theses we

THE FIRST PRINCIPLES OF THE PRACTICAL ORDER 27

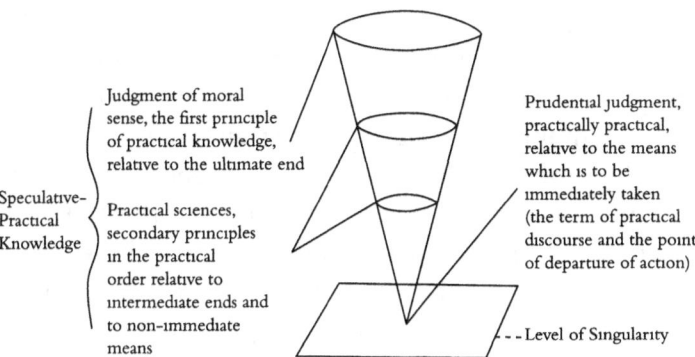

have just formulated. The tip of the cone is a point, thus something irreducible even to the smallest of the circles, which still describes a surface. At the same time, however, as the circles get smaller and smaller toward the tip of the cone, its point, which is a single point, is steadily approximated.

But the really interesting question is: What constitutes the base of the cone? Or, to revert to Aristotle's idiom, what, in the system of practical knowledge, is the first unmoved mover? Now, if we recall that it is finality that gives to practical knowledge its nature, the answer is not all that mysterious. The object of the first principle of practical knowledge will have to be that which is purely and simply *the end* of all human action and with respect to which everything else has the character of means. In other words, the base of the cone represents the judgment of moral sense relative to the ultimate end. And suspended from this base of the primordial moral sense, there stretches a system of practical knowledge, consisting of judgments designed not to determine but to back up that last decision with regard to concrete action, which belongs exclusively to prudence. Again, the base of our cone represents the judgment of the moral sense which bears on that which is purely and simply an end, while its point represents the prudential judgment which bears on that which is purely and simply a means. Moreover, the cross sections parallel to the base can be seen as representing the practical sciences of intermediary ends and non-immediate means, which can be considered less or more practical according as their objects approximate concrete action.

11. Let us understand by 'moral sense' the spiritual quality whereby we grasp the first principles of the practical order, regulative of all practical knowledge. By reason of its scope, the judgment of this moral sense is *speculative-practical* par excellence.[2] It is also an immediate, intuitive judgment, presupposing no discourse. St. Thomas recalls in this connection

---

[2] The position of St. Thomas is well known. While the moral sense (*synderesis*) is not to be identified with the intellectual faculty, it is not a distinct faculty but rather a *habitus* of intelligence. See *Summa theologiae*, Ia, q. 79, aa. 12–13; *Q. D. de veritate*, q. 16, a. 1; John of St. Thomas also holds that moral sense is a *habitus* distinct from that of speculative first principles. *Logica*, II, q. 26, a. 1 (ed. Reiser, p. 794a11). The object of moral sense is not only the first principle of the practical order ("Good should be done and evil avoided"), but any self-evident practical principle; if by preference we speak of the first practical principle, this is because it is the object par excellence of moral sense, as the principle of identity is the object par excellence of the *intellectus principiorum*. Note, too, that a self-evident practical principle can quite easily presuppose a speculative truth which is not self-evident but in need of proof. That God should be honored is an evident practical principle which presupposes certitude about the existence of God, which is not self-evident to us. See John of St. Thomas, *Cursus theologicus*, Ia, disp. 3, a. 1 (ed. Solesmes, I, p. 418b).

the great Dionysian idea that the inferior, in its highest part, participates in the privileges of the superior. Thus, human intelligence, the most elevated part in man's nature, participates, by its grasp of principles, which is the most elevated of its activities, in the privilege of angelic intelligence. In other words, we are entitled to count on intuition in both the practical and the speculative orders, even though between the summit of human thought and the privilege of angelic thought, there remains this difference: that our thought is forever conditioned by sensible experience.[3]

By reason of its immediate character, the judgment of the moral sense may also be called *natural*, since it is right to call natural the data of intellect which in their immediacy are opposed to what is produced by discourse. Indeed, the judgment of moral sense could be said to be natural for an even better reason: springing from the very nature of intelligence it enjoys infallibility.[4]

But, again, it is all-important that we understand precisely in what sense the judgment of moral sense is indefectibly true. Is it indefectibly true with speculative truth, a truth of knowledge, like a scientific judgment, or is there practical truth of direction, supplied by prudential judgment? The answer is not in doubt. Now, in the case of the primordial judgment of the moral sense, I would say that it is indefectibly true both as knowledge and as direction and for these reasons: It is indefectibly true as knowledge because of a perfect adequation with a necessary object—

---

[3] Q. D. *de veritate*, q. 16, aa. 2–3.
[4] Ibid.

namely, that every rational creature is obliged to pursue moral good and avoid moral evil. That is something involving no contingency and susceptible of no defect. Moreover, the judgment of moral sense is indefectibly true also as direction, because it conforms with that love of the absolute good which expresses the very nature of the will.

5

The Movement of Practical Thought

12. Let us turn once more to the text of Aristotle: "[T]hat which is the object of appetite is the stimulant of mind practical; and that which is last in the process of thinking is the beginning of the action."

The end is the desired object; the absolute point of departure of practical intelligence is the end that is only an end, the ultimate end, toward which the will naturally tends and which shapes the judgment of the moral sense. The term of practical discourse is the beginning of action; it is the means that can be put immediately into action, desired conjointly with the end by the good will, and shaped, of course, by prudential judgment. The intermediate steps of practical discourse, rationally organized, are the practical sciences.

13. Like all sciences, practical sciences are specified by the degree of abstraction their objects involve.[1] The different practical sciences answer to different degrees of abstraction, but the whole system of practical knowledge should be characterized, insofar as it is a system of practical knowledge, by a general order of abstraction (within which we should be

---
[1] See John of St. Thomas, *Logica*, II, q. 27, a. 1 (ed. Reiser, p. 822a36) apropos of the distinction of the sciences by way of degrees of abstraction.

able to distinguish degrees). In other words, there should be, from the side of abstraction, a characteristic common to every object of practical knowledge which identifies that object as an object of practical, rather than speculative, knowledge. Whatever that characteristic is, whether practical knowledge at the base or the summit of our cone, or any point in between, it has this objective particularity: that it cannot abstract from existence and implies an essential relation to being effectively posited in existence.[2]

If we were to examine the relation of the speculative sciences to actual existence outside the mind, the following remarks would have to be made:

The case of mathematics must be put to one side since all problems of existence are alien to it, because its object is indifferently a real possible or a mental fiction.

At the opposite extreme, we must set aside the case of God's knowledge, which can never abstract from the problem of existence, because here the essence that is the object of thought is identical with its existence.

And we must also set aside those imperfect parts of the science of nature where, unable to grasp essences with their rational exigencies, we are constrained to grant primacy to observations of fact.

As a rule, the effective positing in existence of any object of thought interests speculative knowledge only *as the indispensable condition of introducing the object of knowledge as essence or as possible.* For example, if I am to know the laws of animal life, it is doubtless

---

[2] John of St. Thomas, *Cursus theologicus, In Iam,* disp. 2, a. 10 (ed. Solesmes, I, p. 395b).

necessary that animals exist, since otherwise I would have no idea of them, but once the idea of animal life with its logical requirements has been disengaged from experience—where it presupposes effective existence—all existent animals could disappear into nothingness without in any way changing my knowledge of animal life. This follows from the very idea of knowledge pure and simple. To know is to become like the object; but as the possible thing was prior to its creation, so is the created thing after receiving the gift of existence. Existence, an accidental attribute in any creature, in no way alters the essence of the nature that it causes to emerge from nothingness, such as it can be, neither more nor less. Existence no more affects the nature of the created thing that is to be posited or not in existence than it affects the essence of a triangle to be drawn by three white lines on a blackboard or by three black lines on white paper.[3] And if this is so, taking into consideration the existence of the (created) thing cannot essentially interest knowledge unless this knowledge is aimed not at its own perfection but at the regulation of an efficient power.

We must, however, explain also the apparent exceptions to this law of speculative thought. As we have said, while mathematics appears wholly indifferent to problems of existence, is it not the case that most other speculative sciences, in some manner, take effective existence into account? Now, mathematics

---

[3] If it is essential to some speculative knowledge, that called intuitive or experimental in the strongest sense, to bear on physical existence, this is so because it is *that* kind of knowledge, not because it is knowledge. See John of St. Thomas, *Logica,* II, q. 23, a. 1 (ed. Reiser, p. 724b14).

is a special case (together with logic), because its object can, without losing anything of its mathematical value, exclude all possibility of extra-mental existence. By contrast, the objects of other speculative sciences include at least a *possibility* of extra-mental existence, which is also why their explanations make use of both efficient and final causality. Notice, however, that the latter are intended not to account for factual existence but only to make known its conditions, so that in these sciences we do not necessarily leave the realm of mere possibility. In the case of knowledge of God, the exception proves the rule; due to the real identity of the divine essence and His existence, one cannot know God as essence, as possible, without knowing Him as existence, as being. Thus, it is in view of playing its role with regard to essence that speculative knowledge is here concerned with the problem of effective existence. As for its imperfectly scientific knowledge where the observation of fact takes the place, for better or worse, of the grasp of essence, it is clear that the primacy of observation answers in it to a defect in the notion of science, to a partial defect of the speculative intellect.[4]

14. The fundamental relation of practical knowledge to the effective existence of its object makes, therefore, for a radical difference between its method of abstraction and that of speculative knowledge. When it is said that practical science proceeds syn-

---

[4] On this subject, see the profound remarks of Édmond Goblot on *logical dualism*, unhappily embedded in a sterile idealism: *Essai sur la classification des sciences* (Paris: F. Alcan, 1898), pp. 14ff., and p. 283: ". . . *pure scientific theory* is not knowledge of reality; it is the construction of systems of relative possibilities."

thetically, *modo compositivo*, unlike speculative science, which proceeds analytically, *modo resolutorio*, the synthesis envisaged is, above all, that of the object of thought and the act of being.[5] Predominance of analysis, predominance of synthesis—such phrases seem too vague to characterize the procedure of scientific thought, but they take on a very clear sense when we consider how the method of practical sciences is affected by the demands of that synthesis.

In fact, the synthesis of the object of thought and the act of being, preeminently characteristic of practical thought, entails, *in the very order of essences*, a synthetic and concretizing procedure proper to practical thought. With an eye to positing something in existence—the term of practical discourse, Aristotle says, is the point of departure of action—practical thought approaches more and more the term for which it is made, and becomes more and more completely itself, to the degree that it has for its object a more completely determined thing. In arriving at its term, practical thought will link up with associative reason (*cogitativa*), which bears on the singular.[6]

It might be objected that such movement of thought in the direction of increasing or diminishing generality is also found in the speculative sciences and is thus in no wise characteristic of practical thought. Consider, for example, the plan of the *Physics* as seen by St. Thomas.[7] First come general treatises dealing

---

[5] See John of St. Thomas, *Cursus theologicus, In Iam*, a. 10 (ed. Solesmes, I, p. 395b); *Logica*, II, 1, a. 4 (ed. Reiser, p. 269b34); Joseph Gredt, *Elementa philosophiae aristotelico-thomisticae*, 2 vols. (Fribourg: Herder, 1909), I, p. 91.

[6] *IaIIae*, q. 47, a. 3, ad 3; Cajetan, *In IamIIae*, q. 57, a. 4.

[7] *In de sensu et sensato*, lectio 1, n. 2.

with the common properties of mobile being (the eight books of the *Physics* of Aristotle), then special treatises ordered according to the increasing complexity of their object (*De coelo et mundo, De generatione et corruptione, De anima* with its continuation, the *Parva naturalia*), on to the histories of plants and animals, where living species are considered in their detail. Doesn't the moralist follow a similar route when after having studied the virtues in general *(IaIIae)* he studies particular virtues *(IIaIIae)* and finally the details of cases of conscience?

The similarity is only apparent. When one moves from the third book of the *Physics* to the little work *De progressu animalium*, one observes indeed a movement of thought toward the concrete but certainly no simultaneous accentuation of its speculative character. In other words, while the mechanism of the progressive movement of reptiles is a more concrete object than the universal laws of movement, a treatise on reptiles is definitely not more speculative than one dealing with physical movement in general. On the contrary, we are tempted to say that it is far less so; or, at least, no one seems to want to argue that it is more *speculative*. But the opposite is true of the practical sciences. Their practical character is accentuated *to the degree that they deal with a more concrete object.* Thus, the *IIaIIae* is more practical than the *IaIIae*, and the moral thought of St. Alphonsus Ligouri is more practical than that of St. Thomas. And the reason why the practical character of practical knowing grows with the concrete character of the object known is precisely that practical thought aims at effecting something in existence. Indeed, this union to be effected between an essence and the act of being determines the peculiar synthetic character of practical thought even in the order of essences, where speculative thought is farthest removed from existence.

15. Thus, from the very point of departure, moral sense gives normative judgment of direction, even though the object of thought is still abstract in the extreme. Then, as it progresses, practical thought adds to itself determination upon determination until, face to face with the singular case, it is ready to be posited in existence. That is what must not be forgotten when we stress the "abstract" character of moral science as compared to the concrete character of prudence. Practical discourse can indeed be conducted at various levels of abstraction, but it always remains through its synthetic method essentially related to existence.[8] If, therefore, it is legitimate to speak of

---

[8] This demand for *total concretion* made by the term of practical discourse also makes prudential judgment radically incommunicable. If there are circumstances in which the conduct I should pursue is clear to all who know my life, there will always be cases where I alone will know what I ought to do, because no one else can know the totality of factors my decision must take into account. That is why, after we have given advice, it is reasonable to refrain from judging one who does not follow it. One who knows enough to give advice does not know enough to tell whether the advice ought to be followed. Putting aside obvious cases, it can be said that advice, even when it is rightly urgent, should always be given with qualifications and especially with the qualification that the last word is with the one who must make the decision. There is an epistemological aberration in the practice of journalists who allow themselves to judge unreservedly in assigning approval or blame to governments, bishops, missionaries, the pope, even to the extent of dictating to them what they must do. The literature of those who reflect on public affairs without themselves being engaged actively would be productive in a quite different way if these arm-

practical science, we must not forget that its generalizations and abstractions, no matter how valid, represent but various stages in a movement of the mind directed from the beginning to a concrete ultimate end.

I have no doubt that it is because this is often forgotten that many moralists suspect all abstract discussions. For instance, several years ago, I found myself one night with some companions at the home of a priest of quite exceptional pastoral gifts; I cannot remember ever having met a more perfect example of the prudent man. The subject of the morality of games of chance arose, and we asked our host if it was legitimate *in itself* to bet a sum of money on a game of cards. He replied by invoking for us the image of ruined families, of health dissipated because of the passion for gambling, suicides at Monte Carlo. Didn't we know that it is not permitted to ruin one's family and one's health, or to expose oneself to the temptation of suicide? Then we asked if money won at gambling is money honestly won. Is the contract,

---

chair advisers understood that their function pertains entirely to the realm of deliberation, and that between deliberation and decision there is a gap that can be adequately appreciated only by the one who must decide. Quite often a priest, pressed by a penitent to provide a ready-made decision, must excuse himself and urge the penitent to assume his own responsibility because only he can know the case completely.

The incommunicability of the prudential judgment sets limits to governing others and provides the basic foundation of personal autonomy. An enlightened despotism therefore may be a contradiction in terms. While it is impossible to set forth in general terms the limits beyond which it is immoral to go in governing others—because of the infinite variety of social circumstances—these limits exist and cannot be arbitrarily altered.

I asked, stipulating that the one who draws the ace of spades takes all the money on the table a licit contract? But there was no way to get a reply. This ideally prudent man refused to consider the question in the abstract, which would require him to dissociate factors that should be considered *all together* by the immediate rule of action, One could say that he exaggerated, for pushed to its logical extreme such an attitude would make moral science impossible. But if this attitude indicates that we are not dealing with a philosopher, it also and more importantly tells us that we are dealing with a man possessed of the proper concern of the moralist.

Thus, the true philosopher-moralist is an extremely rare personage. In him are joined abstractive intelligence, which is the mark of the savant, and that concrete understanding of the contingent singular which is the mark of the prudent man. Such a combination of talents and required suppleness in their interplay surpasses the power of ordinary minds. We expect this of Aristotle, of St. Thomas, of Cajetan. But most moral philosophers succumb to the temptation to "theoritize" about practical affairs.

16. Now, if we compare the orders of practical and speculative knowledge, asking ourselves which speculative abstraction fits the object of thought that practical judgment relates to an end, we note that, even though practical knowledge is fulfilled on a level of concretion alien to all scientific thought, its synthetic movement traverses from top to bottom the orders of abstraction which specify the diverse speculative sciences. Take the first judgment of moral sense: Do good and avoid evil. The logical subject of the judgment is the idea of any rational creature—

abstracted to the third degree; we are within the realm of metaphysics. Take next a law enunciated by moral philosophy: In no case is a man permitted to kill himself. The idea of man is abstract to the first degree; we are at the level of physical science. Finally, I, Job, who have just lost my fortune, my health, my wife: I do not have the right to commit suicide. We have arrived at the level of singular thought, where there is no science and where practical discourse is fulfilled. Only the order of mathematical abstraction, put to one side because its object is but a mental fiction, is skipped by practical discourse. The good is not to be found in mathematics.[9]

17. The reason morals is a philosophical science can now be understood. If it is true that philosophy is preeminently metaphysics, and that every philosophical discipline owes its philosophical character to a systematic research in the light of metaphysics, the practical science of human action is a philosophical science because its supreme regulative principles concern the rational creature. The practical science of dog training is not a philosophical science. But the human will is a spiritual appetite whose nourishment must be sought in the world of transcendentals, in the realm of metaphysics.

---

[9] *Metaphysics*, B, 2, 996a25; M, 3, 1078a31.

6

Moral Philosophy

18. When we move from the self-evident principles formulated by the moral sense to their first scientific determinations, our knowledge changes in kind, as natural and immediate knowledge gives way to demonstrative knowledge, acquired by an effort of mind. Similarly, when we move from the last practical judgment in universal matter to a practical judgment in singular matter, our scientific knowledge, whose justification depends on anterior knowledge, gives way to prudential knowledge, justified by the inclination of the virtuous will, or *affective connaturality*. The question is whether, between the first scientific determinations of practical knowledge and the last practical judgment in universal matter, that is, within the limits defined by the base of our cone and its summit, there is also diversity of knowledge.

To this question, Jacques Maritain, in a recent study,[1] gives the following answer. There are two sorts of practical science, distinguished not only by an unequal degree of abstraction, but even more by a fundamental difference in the mode of knowing that they bring into play. There is a *speculatively practical* science, represented, as far as human action is concerned, by moral philosophy as one finds it, for example, in the work of St. Thomas, and a *practically*

---

[1] "St. John of the Cross, Practitioner of Contemplation," in *The Degrees of Knowledge*, pp. 329–74.

practical science, examples of which we find in the teaching of St. John of the Cross or St. Alphonsus Ligouri. The complete scheme of the system of practical knowledge will thus comprise, between the judgment of the moral sense and that of prudence, two stages of knowledge distinct in type.²

Not only is this distinction of two unequal types of practical knowing indispensable, we think, for understanding the true significance of the teaching of a mystic like St. John of the Cross, but it also supplies a precious aid for understanding the scientific character of moral philosophy.

19. The most considerable logical treatise to which the Aristotelian school gave birth is the incomparable *Ars logica* of John of St. Thomas. It contains, by way of short asides, the sketch of a theory of

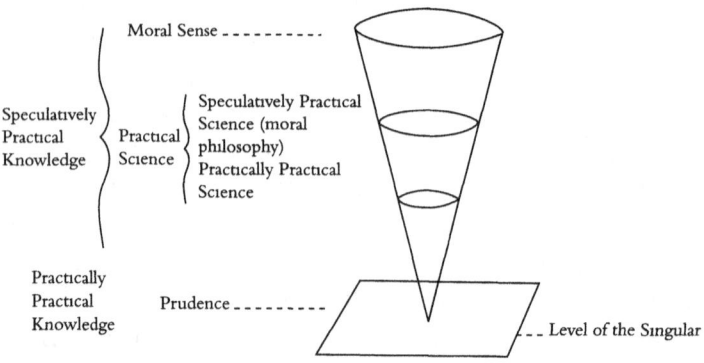

---

² A question of terminology: it might seem shocking that a science called *practically practical* should be included under *speculatively practical* knowledge; there is a subtlety here that seems absolutely necessary if we are to safeguard the indisputable principle that all scientific knowledge, since it must have the universal for its object, remains to some degree speculative, and that only prudence and art represent knowledge that is *absolutely practical*.

moral philosophy. It is a characteristic solution of the problem, which, because it is the work of a thinker of genius who is celebrated for his customary fidelity to the teachings of Aristotle and St. Thomas, calls for careful examination.

By moral science, John of St. Thomas suggests, we can mean not simply the science of morals, but a whole constituted of moral science and prudence. So understood, moral science is practical because it includes prudence and thus makes use of the principle *The good must be done* in a practical manner. But if moral science is taken apart from prudence, it is a speculative science, and this is clear in the *Prima Secundae*. In this science, principles do not at all function in a practical manner, that is, as source of an affective movement or engagement of the heart. They are, in fact, speculative principles whose only function is to make known the nature of the virtues as pure objects of thought, and it is thus, our author repeats and makes precise, that things are presented both in the *Ethics* and in the whole of the *Prima Secundae*.

Now, it follows from this that there is no practical science, since moral science can be called practical only insofar as it is conjoined with prudence and *by reason of the prudence that accompanies it*. Nor does he think it absurd that there is no practical science that is properly a science, since science proceeds by way of analysis and definition and the practical by moving and composing.[3] Elsewhere John writes, "If one speaks of moral science in a practical sense, it is identical with prudence. . . . if one speaks of it in a speculative sense, understanding by this the ethical science

---

[3] *Logica*, II, q. 1, a. 4 (ed. Reiser, p. 276b34).

that treats the virtues, it belongs to the philosophy of nature, which studies the rational soul and ought, accordingly, to study moral acts."[4]

Father Joseph Gredt, always a loyal follower of John of St. Thomas, comments on this doctrine as follows. "A science, properly speaking, is always a purely speculative *habitus*, and any science called practical is either art . . . or prudence. That is why ethics, if it does not include prudence, is itself a speculative science. In fact, in order for there to be a practical science, or practical *habitus*, it is not enough that the object considered be a matter for action; it is also necessary that it be considered in a practical manner. Thus, it is only in a large sense, and insofar as it treats of an object that is a matter for action, that ethics can be called a practical science."[5] But of course, in this large sense, ethics is only accidentally practical; in the strict sense, it remains essentially speculative.[6]

Since an accident cannot play the role of specifying it, it follows that moral philosophy is purely and simply a speculative science and a stranger in its essential line to the motion of desire; it is only a psychology of virtues. Now, this position is inspired by a firm resolve to safeguard the originality of the notion of practical knowledge, which leads to the unwillingness to call practical any knowledge which would be only accidentally so. For sure, if moral science, as it is treated in the *Ethics* and in the *Prima Secundae*, in-

---

[4] Ibid., II, q. 27, a. I (ed. Reiser, I, p. 826b44). See *The Material Logic of John of St. Thomas*, trans. Yves R. Simon, John J. Glanville, and G. Donald Hollenhorst (Chicago: The University of Chicago Press, 1955), p. 564.

[5] Gredt, *Elementa philosophiae thomisticae*, I, 93.

[6] Ibid., 207.

volves no procedure proper to practical knowledge, governed by that which is the function of practical knowledge—namely, the motion of desire—it is completely speculative in its status as science. But is it true that moral science, insofar as it does not include prudence, involves no procedure proper to practical knowledge? It is this that seems highly questionable.

In fact, I detect a certain vacillation in the exposition of John of St. Thomas. What he gives as an example of speculative moral science, in the *Summa theologiae*, is the *Prima Secundae* alone, as if recognizing that the *Secunda Secundae* is something else. That is what gives pause, and the least one can say is that the thought of the author comprises some obscurity. Moreover, he also gives all of the *Ethics* as an example of speculative science of moral matters, which does not seem to be what Aristotle had in mind, or how St. Thomas judged the work of Aristotle. From whatever distance, they are both intent on directing action, or, at the very least, on motivating the reader to take a personal interest in moral matters.

In this science, St. Thomas writes in the prologue to his commentary on the *Ethics*, one applies universal and simple principles to particular cases where action takes place. "In fact, one must in every practical [*operativa*] science proceed by way of synthesis, whereas by contrast in speculative sciences one must proceed by way of analysis, resolving the complex into simple principles. Afterward, one must show the truth *by way of images*, that is, under a likely guise, and to do so is to proceed *according to the proper principles of this science*. For moral science has human acts for its object, and *what moves the will is not only the good but also the apparent good*."

20. Thus, for St. Thomas, moral philosophy displays the synthetic method characteristic of practical knowledge, and must measure its procedures according to the exigencies of the movement of desire that constitutes, according to Aristotle, its end. We are far from that speculative science defined by John of St. Thomas, analytic in method and a stranger to the reactions of will. Must we say that St. Thomas is explaining Aristotle and not giving his own doctrine? The terms of the commentary seem to exclude this hypothesis. It is easier to agree that John of St. Thomas, against his usual practice, departs here from the thought of his master without, however, showing any awareness that he is doing so.

21. We have seen that the judgment of moral sense implies agreement with a certain desire, the natural desire by which will is drawn by its object. At the same time as it is speculatively true by conformity with reality, the judgment of moral sense, relative to the absolute end, is practically true in conformity with the natural impetus of will to the good. At the opposite extreme, the prudential judgment, relative to the immediate means, which may not be speculatively true, however it tries to be, is practically true by conformity with the virtuous movement of will whose just direction to the absolute end envelops the acceptance of the means required to attain the end. Thus, at both the base and the summit of the cone, there is an effective commensuration of knowledge with desire, the actual proportion of the act of knowing and the act of love, and it is the actuality of this proportion or commensuration that confers on the moral sense and on prudence their practical character.

It is clear that things are not like this in moral philosophy. One can recognize that such an end should be taken as the end of will in certain circumstances without feeling the actual desire for that end. For example, I can recognize that one should render to each his due and feel no inclination to pay my debts. But it is not about this that one disputes: what is asked is whether moral philosophy has for its function to inspire the effective desire for the good or only to make natural finalities known in the way that physics and metaphysics make natures known, that is, in a purely speculative manner. But the first hypothesis perfectly represents the thought of Aristotle that advises adolescents and people troubled by their passions not to take a course in moral philosophy. A man who is the slave of his passions might perhaps agree that the maxims formulated by moral philosophy correctly express the finalities inscribed in the free agent, but his personal life will not be bettered because he lacks the proper end of moral philosophy, which is not knowledge but action.[7] If moral philosophy has for its end to direct action, however remotely, it is properly practical knowledge and it occurs, as we admitted in a provisory way, on the descending axis which goes from the judgment of moral sense to the judgment of prudence. It is a determination of what the judgment of moral sense has left vague, not only in that it makes us know in a manner already precise and detailed the nature of the good the free agent should desire, but also in the sense that it is essentially made to provoke, in a way measured by its precision, a new interest of desire.

---

[7] *Ethics*, I.1.1095a4. The simple truth is that ethics considers the right and the wrong of human *use*; this is distinct from the consideration of natural finalities in theoretical science.

To be sure, one cannot deny that there exists a kind of purely speculative knowledge of human finalities. But that is not moral philosophy as Aristotle understood it. By assigning to it a motivating role, Aristotle ruled out the possibility of moral philosophy's ever becoming a purely speculative science of human finalities. Surely we need to know what is good for man not only at the concrete level of individual action but also at the intelligible plane of essences. But we cannot grasp the idea of the just end for man except in a form that stirs up desire for the same just end. We understand well how those who wish to safeguard the autonomy of the more proximate and especially of the immediate rules of action are reluctant to grant to the more remote and abstract proposition of moral philosophy an efficacious motivating role. But let us at the same time point out that such a radical defense of one part of practical thought, adapted to the contingencies and complexities of human action, threatens not only to empty the rest of it of most of its intelligibility but also to deprive that action of most of its spirituality.[8] Taking such risks is not necessary from a correct Aristotelian point of view. The danger of theory or speculative science encroaching upon issues that can be settled only by prudential judgment is virtually eliminated from moral philosophy precisely to the degree that it adapts to its motivating role. A moral philosophy that takes its role to be not only to try to define essences and finalities but also to inspire interest in the good will never forget that the end toward which it is directed is not for it to reach

---

[8] See Garrigou-Lagrange, "Le réalisme moral, la finalité, et la formation de la conscience" in *Le réalisme du principe de finalité*, pp. 285–99.

in concrete action. And so, instead of pushing for application of general *a priori* rules, this philosophy will openly recognize that its maxims are true only in most cases and will therefore carefully surround them with appropriate reservations, restrictions, and exceptions as befits general rules of human action.

Again, if moral philosophy were totally without a motivating role, it would be rather incongruous to claim rationality for human conduct. To act fully as human beings, we need a practical light emanating from the intelligible depth of things. And provided that we understand what its motivating role implies, there is little danger that universal-practical thought should stifle the free development of those additional qualities of character upon which singular-practical thought depends exclusively for correct decisions in concrete actions.

Finally, since we really cannot live without philosophy altogether, if we denied the practical and motivating character to moral philosophy, we would have to turn for general rules for our actions to some sort of completely speculative science of human finalities. But such a science is not organized along an axis that allows it to descend from metaphysical abstraction to the level of concrete action; nor has such science any use for the synthetic method which makes sense of practical discourse in real life. Indeed, no speculative science is fit to handle the irreducible uniqueness of singular cases, and as soon as it tries to go beyond certain general principles, it clearly runs the risk of ruining action by existentially irrelevant truths. But if there are moral philosophies that the man of action rightly mistrusts, there is also moral philosophy that knows how to adapt its scientific procedures to its motivating function.

7
Practically Practical Science

22. The distinction Maritain draws between a speculatively practical science and a practically practical science is justified by the very application in view of which it appears to have been made. By employing this distinction, its author solves with admirable lucidity difficulties that arise from the confrontation of formulas of St. Thomas with those of St. John of the Cross. Whatever the future reception of the idea sketched in the work of Maritain, we believe that it represents, for the theory of practical knowledge, a definitive contribution.

Certain critics have feared that the definition of a practically practical science distinct from moral philosophy leads to too speculative a conception of the latter. We do not share this fear, *salvo meliori judicio*. To call moral philosophy a *speculatively practical* science is not to misunderstand its practical character in the way John of St. Thomas does. In order for the proposed distinction to be seen as absolutely necessary it suffices that, at a certain stage, still scientific, not yet prudential, of its development, practical thought use concepts elaborated according to laws that do not belong either to speculative science or to moral philosophy.

> In the first place, the most important thing to note is that the sciences which we have called *practically practical* make a wholly different use of concepts than do

the *speculative* or *speculatively practical* sciences; not only as to their determining finalities and procedure in discourse, but also as to the manner in which the concepts themselves are fashioned and recast, signify and grasp the real and, if I may so speak, make intelligible cross-sections of things. Let us say that in the speculative sciences concepts have their bare abstractive and intelligible value. In these sciences the question is to analyze the real into its ontological or empiriological elements. In the practical sciences, on the contrary, concepts incorporate a whole progression of concrete harmonics; here the question is to assemble the means, the dynamic moments by which action comes into existence. Whence it follows that in these two orders of knowledge concepts that have the same name (one of which is the projection of the other into another noetic sphere) are differently related to the real.[1]

Speculative knowledge provides us with the best example to exhibit what a difference of *conceptual registers* is. The concepts that the philosophy of nature uses have for their function to make known *what* sensible things *are*; the concepts used by the empiriological science of nature have for their purpose to give us, with respect to these same things, a formula clearly translatable into sensations. Whereas for philosophy the best definition is that which is most easily resolved into the idea of being as being, for the scientist the best definition is that which evokes the most clearly discernible sensations, so much so that the scientist rightly prefers an imperfect and rough definition to a perfect definition of the philosophical kind. In empiriological science the law of resolution into

---

[1] *The Degrees of Knowledge,* p. 346.

the observable governs all the activities of thought, and to remain faithful to that law one does not hesitate to surrender the advantage of superior intelligibility.[2]

Something analogous happens in practical knowledge. The moral philosopher—and we have seen how he suspends the chain of his deductions from the heaven of metaphysical abstraction—is concerned to confer the maximum intelligibility on rules of action and consequently holds himself to a *speculatively exact* analysis of the real. The ideas he forms of the substance of the soul, of its faculties, of will and sensible desire, for example, do not differ from those fashioned by the psychologist. The development of his thought, the procedures put in play in his demonstrations may differ profoundly from the method followed in speculative science, but it is still true that *at the outset* he must approach speculatively every kind of cause whose exercise constitutes the world of morality. Indeed, this is the main source of the difficulties we mentioned earlier concerning the precise role of the moral philosopher. He is often ill at ease because, even though concerned with the efficacious

---

[2] For example: "Variability of behavior, adapted to complex circumstances of the moment and benefiting from the acquisitions of experience, is a criterion of what is called intelligence, as opposed to the fixed characteristics and the automatic responses of instinct by heredity." Henri Pieron, *Psychologie experimentale* (Paris: Armand Colin, 1934), p. 35. "The distinctive sign of intelligence can only be the progressive adaptation to the surrounding environment, which translates modifications introduced into the nerve centers." Howard C. Warren, *Précis de psychologie* (Paris: M. Rivière, 1923), p. 123. What can a philosopher make of these definitions of intelligence? Nothing, except to notice that they are not philosophical definitions.

direction of action, he must use a method whose first law is fidelity to ontological reality. The moral philosopher cannot escape the law of analysis which dissociates *what* the natures envisaged *are* from *what they are not*, even while he is committed to the higher law of synthesis, that is, of putting together *all* the factors necessary for the integrity of the moral act. Thus, it is inevitable that, in the descent of practical thought toward the absolute concrete, a moment comes when the demands of the proximate guidance of action become totally incompatible with those of ontological analysis, and that is when the role of the philosopher is finished. Under no pretext can he as philosopher renounce speculative analysis, which alone can resolve concepts into the idea of being, the condition of the philosophical character of thought. And so, just as in speculative science the philosopher gives way to the scientist when going further into the detail of sensible things calls for the renunciation of definitions resoluble into the idea of being, so in practical science when it becomes impossible to satisfy the demands of direction without renouncing the use of ontologically exact definitions, the moral philosopher gives way to the moral practitioner. Let us take some examples from Maritain:

> St. John of the Cross describes contemplation as *non-agere*, whereas St. Thomas defines it as the *highest activity*. And yet they agree with each other. One takes the ontological point of view, and from this point of view, there is no higher activity than to adhere vitally to God by infused love and infused contemplation, under the influence of operating grace. The other takes the point of view of mystical experience itself, and from this point of view, the suspension of every

activity in the *human mode* appears to the soul as non-activity. Not to move oneself, to cease from all particular operation, to be in supreme act of attentive and loving immobility, which is itself received from God—is this not to do nothing, not, of course, in the ontological sense, but in the psychological and practical meaning of the word?[3]

So, too, when St. John of the Cross says "that certain divine touches . . . are experienced in the very substance of the soul, as opposed to its powers or faculties," the word 'substance' is not to be understood in the philosopher's sense:

> For him, the question bears on the degrees of interiority of the divine operations. And when divine action, having first touched the substance of the soul, touches the faculties in their deepest roots and they, being thus supernaturally moved, become so spiritualized that they allow a glimpse of the soul's depths to shine through, as it were, then it is not the naked substance which acts or knows by itself; the soul does indeed know and act by its powers, and by the gifts and infused love, but in so intimate a center—at the secret nexus where the soul's powers are rooted—that no particular action is produced by these powers, which are actuated from their very depths *in darkness and in concealment,* and absolutely no sign indicates to the angels what is going on in the deepest recesses of the heart.[4]

So again, St. John of the Cross, like the majority of mystics, constantly makes use of the Augustinian division of the higher faculties into *understanding, memory and will.* . . . And actually—even though from

---

[3] *The Degrees of Knowledge,* pp. 347–48.
[4] Ibid., pp. 348–49.

the point of view of speculative and ontological analysis the bipartite division into *intellect* and *will* is the only one conformed to the real—from the point of view of practical analysis, which distinguishes the powers of the soul not according to their essential ontological articulations, but according to the subject's principal concrete modes of activity with respect to his ends, the Augustinian division is the right one, it is this division that is in conformity with reality, with *that* reality.[5]

When we consider the nature of things, it is not true that infused contemplation is a state of non-acting, or that a feeling has the substance of the soul for its immediate subject, or that intellectual memory is a faculty distinct from intelligence. But for one occupied not with the nature of things but with the transcendent infused contemplation itself, it is different. Here it is right to conceive thought as a kind of rest, mystical feelings as touching the very substance of the soul, and intellectual memory as a distinct faculty. Such a way of thinking is as legitimate as that of empiriological science when it formulates definitions that, from an ontological point of view, would be false or even absurd. But whereas the empiriological concept departs from the philosophical concept in virtue of a still quite speculative need, the practically practical concept departs from it out of a practical requirement.

23. This leads us to ask what is the relation of practical truth, or the truth of direction, to speculative truth, or the truth of knowledge, in the two kinds of practical science.

---

[5] Ibid., p. 351.

We have seen that in the prudential judgment speculative truth and practical truth do not always necessarily coincide. Recall the example of the heir who doubts his titles. He can have no certainty of conscience unless he does his best to verify the legitimacy of his possession. But if, having done this, he still has no total proof, what is he supposed to do? We suggested that it would be right for him to retain his fortune, even though in reality it might have been amassed by a long since forgotten swindle. Thus, the same judgment, "I am right to retain my fortune," could be practically true and speculatively false.

But, as we have also seen, as far as the primordial judgment of moral sense is concerned, there is no disassociation between the truth of knowledge and the truth of guidance. Here we need to add that this goes for any maxim enunciated by moral philosophy, insofar as it retains its scientific character and does not try to decide singular cases. For example, the rule that "All merchandise ought to be sold at a just price which cannot be arbitrarily determined" is true by conformity with an objective law as well as by conformity with the inclination of the virtuous will.

Difficulties arise in the case of practically practical science, which is also supposed to keep theoretical and practical truth together. The prudent man, without betraying prudence, may give advice that in the event, new facts obtaining, turns out to be unfortunate. He has erred speculatively but not practically, since under obligation to give it he gave the best advice he could. But the moral practitioner who aspires to *scientific* direction of conduct has no business formulating a maxim that may turn out to be disastrous.⁶ Innocent insofar as he is a man, he would sin as a scientist. Thus, if a disassociation between speculative and practical truth is at all possible in this most practical of the practical sciences, it is only in a very weak sense, in which one speaks of truth in the first operation of the mind. A practically true concept, as distinguished from a practical decision, can be speculatively false only in the sense in which a concept empiriologically true can be ontologically false. But, the practical concept once given, the scientific judgment in which it figures cannot be true by conformity with well-ordered desire without at the same time being true by conformity with reality, that is, without expressing a real property of the reality we have chosen to express, according to a choice ruled, not by the demands of knowledge, but by those of guidance.

---

⁶ Unless the disaster is due to an error of interpretation, in which case the author of a practically practical piece remains innocent both as scientist and as man. The practically practical genre is particularly open to erroneous interpretations because of the perfectly understandable tendency to understand in a speculative sense what is meant in a quite practical one. The works of the most orthodox mystics have often given rise to pantheistic, Manichean, or quietist deviations that warn us that reading them requires a definite preparation.

8
Christian Ethics

24. Thus far we have been considering the problem of practical knowledge as it appears to the pure philosopher. We have assumed that the supreme regulative and moving science of human action is moral philosophy, and when we appealed to the example of theological works, such as the *Summa* of St. Thomas and the commentaries of St. John of the Cross, we considered only what they have in common with works of a profane character, analogous to them in scientific procedure. This is a logician's abstraction that ceases to be legitimate if one means to do the theory of practical knowledge practically. The prudence that ought actually to be the immediate guide of Christian conduct is not the natural virtue described by Aristotle but a supernatural virtue. The speculatively practical science that should provide the general principles of the Christian's action is not philosophy but theology, and the only practitioners whose maxims should be fully welcome to him are the saints.[1]

---

[1] See the collective work *Clairvoyance de Rome* (Paris: Spes, 1929), pp. 225ff. "And it is impossible that the political science and prudence of a Christian should be *the same* as those of a pagan (even supposing, which is not the case with [Charles] Maurras, that he knows God by reason). Only the Christian is capable of a political science and prudence adapted to the governance of fallen and redeemed men" (p. 230).

One cannot insist too much that the relation of natural knowledge to revealed varies essentially depending on whether it is a matter of speculative knowledge or practical knowledge. If it were simply a matter of knowing for the sake of knowing, what is seen to be true by natural reason is definitively so, and revelation can in no wise change it. It is true, as Étienne Gilson has reminded us,[2] that the influence faith exercises on the existential activity (*travail vécu*) of the metaphysician may help his science achieve perfection. But faith enters into the labors of the metaphysician only to make up for his own insufficiency. Otherwise, with or without the aid of faith, the results of metaphysical research free of error, if they are such as can be complete, permit no altering and can be incorporated *as such* into the synthesis of Christian wisdom. The theological knowledge of the triune God is added to the philosophical knowledge of the one God, without in any way modifying what philosophy has demonstrated concerning the one God. If we consider not the concrete exercise of thought but its essential determinations, the revealed novelty, in speculative matter, supervenes by way of pure *addition*.

It is quite otherwise in practical matters. Christian ethics exercises far more control and influence on moral philosophy than Christian dogma exercises on metaphysics. A moral system erected without knowledge of what only revelation can tell us would suppose that human nature is in fact endowed with all the powers a man should have for a perfectly healthy

---

[2] *The Spirit of Mediaeval Philosophy*, trans. A. H. C. Downes (New York: Charles Scribner's Sons, 1940).

nature. But we know that human nature was not only despoiled by original sin of the supernatural gifts that God had gratuitously conferred upon it in the state of innocence, but also *wounded*. A man was traveling from Jerusalem to Jericho and was set upon by robbers who not only took his money and clothes but also injured him in such a way that they left him incapable of helping himself. The man the Good Samaritan gratuitously cared for is sinful humanity. Let us not speak of our capacities as if original sin had not left us in a ditch from which only divine grace can rescue us.

Moreover and above all it is clear that every alteration in the end to be pursued entails an alteration in the means adapted to it. A purely natural ethics is constructed with an eye to a natural ultimate end, and in that perspective the just mean where virtue resides is determined with respect to that end. But revelation makes known to us that man is in fact destined to a supernatural end. This supernatural ultimate end, and the means God has fashioned for its attainment, not only create absolutely new obligations, such as the frequent reception of the sacraments, but also change, at least in some cases, the rule of obligations already formulated by natural reason. Thus it is, according to the classic example, that a purely natural wisdom, though it prescribes sobriety, disapproves of all extreme forms of asceticism. We think that no philosophy could by means of simple philosophical principles, justify the mortifications of a St. Catherine of Siena. For the Christian, on the contrary, who knows the supernatural efficacy of penance, the most naturally painful forms of asceticism are licit under certain conditions and sometimes obligatory.³

Thus, not only is it impermissible for the Christian to remain on the level of natural ethics, but, contrary to the case of speculative truth where he can live with the conclusions of natural metaphysics, the Christian cannot even accept natural ethics except as revised in the light of revelation.⁴

Hence, the extreme difficulty of collaboration, which is nonetheless necessary, between the believer and the non-believer in matters where human ends are directly involved. In a city where minds are divided it is necessary that Christians work with non-Christians for the common good of the city, but in the matter of the ideas directive of political life their agreement can be only partial. It is impossible that the ideas they have in common could have the character of a complete political doctrine. Whereas the Christian and the non-Christian can be in perfect accord on a system of speculative truths, no system concerned with the general moral conduct could receive the complete agreement of the Christian and the non-Christian. Agreement can be had only on lim-

---

³ *IaIIae*, q. 63, a. 4.

⁴ No purely natural moral system can be completely true, because it is essential to moral philosophy that it take the existential conditions of humanity into account. It remains to be seen if any Christian moral science is in essence theological, or if, still necessarily subordinated to theology, it can be conceived as distinct from it in its scientific formality and in its methods. Maritain recently set forth with great effect the notion of a Christian moral philosophy distinct from theology in *An Essay on Christian Philosophy* (trans. Edward H. Flannery [New York: Philosophical Library, 1955]). The idea is quite new, open to discussion, and we do not mean to take a stand on it now.

ited points, where it will always be necessary to see the limits clearly and frankly. It may even be permissible, moreover, to think that the relative *separation* thus imposed on the Christian contributes better to fruitful collaboration than would the kind of confusion pleasing to empirical minds.

9
Moral Philosophy and the Science of Moral Acts

25. Sacred or profane moral science, even speculatively practical, is only in small part a matter of pure deduction. In reasoning about the essence of man without having any recourse to experience, one can come up with only a small number of rules of an extreme generality and scarcely capable of moving desire. As soon as one wishes to descend to some detail and determine the means (even still quite general ones remote from immediate action) necessary to attain the ends assigned by way of rational deduction, it is necessary to observe men acting and to measure the results of their conduct on a scale of the ends rationally assigned to human conduct. Why does conduct of a certain kind produce a result conformed to such an end? Most of the time we cannot say. Moral philosophy, which must explain, rationally justify, the ends that it proposes, as soon as it turns to the designation of means, is in large measure only a science of *observation*. Why are lusts allayed when one resists them? It would be a clever man who could say. Syllogizing about lust, one would conclude with some probability that resistance exasperates lust, but experience shows the contrary to be the case. Deduction allows us to assert that the state has the obligation to look out for public health, as it has to take measures to diminish crime. Given that, one might, for

example, ask if the use of alcoholic beverages should be completely prohibited. That is a matter of experience, so let us try to observe and understand what happened in America as a result of Prohibition.

To the degree that it is aware of its experimental character, moral philosophy will avoid dogmatism, so repugnant to the needs of practical thought. Experience teaches us in fact that with respect to the same end what is good for some is bad for others, with the result that universal and unchangeable moral doctrine amounts to a few precepts of extremely high generality. As soon as it is a question of making duties precise, moral philosophy can formulate laws only of frequency, open to numerous exceptions. Apart from pathological cases, due to corruption of conscience under the influence of bad use of freedom, there is room, in the system of human conduct, for innumerable legitimate and reasonable variations, due quite simply to the concrete variety of the conditions in which the problem of human salvation poses itself.[1]

It is indeed unfortunate that when modern sociological studies revealed that one can interpret differently the moral values cherished by the European bourgeoisie of the nineteenth century without perverting them, moral philosophy was represented in our schools by an official and conformist doctrine too little concerned with experience. But in order to

---

[1] See the remarkable prologue to Aristotle's *Ethics*, so well understood by St. Thomas, but interpreted by Paul Janet in terms characteristic of the theorist who does not understand the role of experience in ethics. *Histoire de la science politique*, ed. Georges Picot, 3d ed., 2 vols. (Paris: F. Alcan, 1900), I, pp. 166–67, 189. See *In I Ethic,* lectio 3; *In V Ethic.*, lectio 12; *IaIIae*, q. 91, a. 4; q. 97, a. 1; q. 104, a. 3, ad l.

knock down the proud edifice of this ethics of professors, a few grenades fired by other professors sufficed.

26. A system of moral philosophy must include a vast repertory of factual observations, which is an indispensable annex of practical discourse. A treatise on politics, for example, must include careful studies of the actual life of societies. Manuals of sociology are pleased to recognize in the great political philosophers of the past the precursors of sociology. And *with reason*. It was indeed necessary that representatives of *normative politics* be sociologists before the word existed; otherwise they would not have been genuine political philosophers, but only dreamers of utopias. Thus, the necessity, for moral philosophy and especially for politics, of a science of social facts cannot be stressed enough. But neither can we let certain claims by contemporary sociologists go unchallenged. Many of them pretend that their science is something other than an annex of a moral and political philosophy and that it enjoys, with respect to them, complete independence. In fact, not only do they pretend that sociology is a positive science, analogous, despite the originality so solicitously claimed for its method, to the natural sciences; but its bolder exponents, who today are legion, even pretend that it can become a *rational moral art* founded on new supreme principles of morality.

Now, what should be clear to everyone is that a science of social facts, constructed in indifference to every value judgment yet producing a system of practical rules susceptible of obliging the will, would be nothing short of a miracle. We know that what makes the construction of medical art and science, on the basis of scientific knowledge of pathological facts, possible is the unanimous agreement on the end of medicine, the curing of sickness. Likewise, a study of the fact of suicide, by making known the conditions under which suicides are most frequent, makes sense only as long as one presupposes that one should not commit suicide. So, too, it must be presupposed that it is always better to conserve life than to cause death. But this is a presupposition that a factual science that avoids the light of every judgment of value or of natural finality can never establish.

Thus, the real problem, in our view, is not whether sociology is capable of founding a new morality, but rather whether sociology can ever be totally independent of the principles formulated by the practical science of human action. We simply do not think that a completely speculative science of social facts indifferent to all human values is possible. Can one, for example, make a scientific study of facts concerning economic life without making any value judgments about, say, the best conception of work and money, taking into account the variations called for by the variety of conditions? We do not think that possible. And that is why we must also object to the compromising attitude taken by some resolute critics of the more outrageous claims of the contemporary sociological movement who, while most firmly attached to the true notion of a normative moral philosophy, concede without a second thought that a sociology independent of every moral system is both possible and desirable, provided that such a sociology refrain from turning itself into an ethics or substituting itself for moral philosophy.[2]

---

[2] See J.-T. Delos, "L'Objet de la sociologie", in the collective work, *Comment juger la sociologie contemporaine* (Marseilles: Éditions Publiroc, n.d.).

The truth of the matter is that sociology needs practical light because of the character of its object. For it is only by postulating a fundamental negation of all freedom in human action that social facts can be purged of all moral considerations, and that is something no sociologist has yet managed to do.[3]

So the object of sociology remains essentially moral being, which is a reality constituted by a good or bad use of liberty.[4] To act as a human being is to act consciously toward a known end, and this action more than just implies a moral value. No matter how identical they may appear externally, *a morally good action is not the same thing as a morally bad action*. Thus, in moral matters there are *no judgments of reality without judgments of value*. Consequently, any science having moral being for its object is constrained, under penalty of falsifying the nature of its object, to work in the light of moral philosophy, which knows the ends of human action.

A recent book on present-day Germany provides a nice example of this necessity for practical judgments of value to make sense of social facts, which are moral facts. In a passage reporting on the actual state of sexual morality in the large cities of Germany, Pierre Viénot recounts the following observations: *first*, a special importance is no longer attached to a young woman's being a virgin; *second*, contraceptive practices are generally considered legitimate; *third*, homo-

---

[3] In making this affirmation, we have in mind only the *aggregate* and principal parts of the sociological discipline; in no way do we deny that certain secondary objects studied by sociology can in their scientific conception be indifferent to morality and take on the character of simply natural objects.

[4] By 'moral being' we understand here not the subject capable of morality (man), but the moral act itself and everything defined with reference to it. See the following chapter.

sexuality more and more loses its character as a shameful vice, and weighty opinion calls for the abrogation of the law that considers it a crime. Now, regardless of whether or not he got his facts right, the author, conscious or not of conforming to the true method of sociology, lets us immediately know also that, in his own judgment, "it is a mistake to interpret them as a sign of increasing immorality. To my mind," he writes, "they reveal a permanent change in the boundaries of morality, the retreat of Christian morality, and a profound modification of the spirit in which the nineteenth century approached these questions."[5] And that is precisely our point. A fact like the inclusion of homosexuality in the mores of a society and its acceptance by the collective conscience becomes intelligible and can be explained only by reference to the question of whether or not it is "a sign of increasing immorality." In order to agree on the intelligibility of social facts, one cannot be in disagreement about their value.[6]

Now, one might still argue that the sociologist, while not understanding facts in the same way as the moralist does, is nonetheless able to acquire some correct understanding of them. All he does is to abstract from moral values, leaving to others the task of judging. Thus, even though his object may be incomplete, it does not have to be necessarily miscon-

---

[5] Pierre Viénot, *Is Germany Finished?* (New York: Macmillan, 1932), p. 40.

[6] On this idea that in moral matters a scientific understanding of factual observations is possible only in the light of a practical science making known *what moral things ought to be*, see the forceful pages of Daniel Lallement in *Clairvoyance de Rome*, pp. 178ff.

ceived. For, after all, as the old adage has it, abstraction is not deception. But let us be cautious here. Abstraction is not deception on the condition that it does not destroy the object it seeks to isolate; otherwise it can be fatal to understanding. In the admirable passage where he sets forth the theory of two kinds of abstraction, abstraction of the universal whole and abstraction of formal determinations, which leaves aside the given material, St. Thomas shows that in both cases what makes abstraction legitimate is that the abstracted object does not imply in its intelligible essence (*ratio*) that from which abstraction is made.[7] Thus, the genus animal can be considered in abstraction from the characteristics proper to man, because the concept of animal does not include rationality. But one cannot think man without thinking animal. Likewise, quantity can be considered in abstraction from every sensible quality, but sensible quality cannot be understood in abstraction from quantity. Now, what we want to know is simply whether it is legitimate for us to consider the social fact in abstraction from morality in the same way as we consider "animal" and "quantity" in abstraction from "human" and "sensible quality." We know that we cannot think morality without thinking society. But can we think society without thinking morality? Or would such dissociation destroy our understanding of the social fact? The answer is not in doubt. For instance, no sociologist would deny that two acts absolutely identical in their natural being, say, the marital act and fornication, are not *sociologically* different. The institution of marriage is an important

---

[7] *In Boëthii de Trinitate*, q. 5, a. 1.

datum for the sociologist, and how people behave in and out of it makes a difference in his study and findings. But, clearly, there would be no sociological significance to the difference between the marital act and fornication were these not first of all morally different. In other words, as social facts these acts do more than just imply what they are "abstracted" from, which renders their abstraction invalid. Without an understanding of their moral signification they have no sociological meaning.[8]

27. If these views are well founded, it would appear that for a discipline to be properly classified as a moral science it is not necessary for it to aim at guiding action; it is enough for it to have a moral reality for its object. True, it would be an abuse of language to extend the term 'moral science' to every discipline that studies a being capable of moral life. For instance, taken as a whole, psychology needs to be classified as a natural science, because its proper object is not the operation of free causes but the play of natural causes.

---

[8] We have yet to ask whether non-normative social science, and above all sociology, should be seen as specifically distinct from ethics or as simple addenda to it. Without presuming to settle the matter, I can give it as my opinion that the distinction formulated by Cajetan (*In Iam*, q. 14, a. 16) between the *end of the knowledge* and the *end of the knower* is important here. The end pursued by the sociologist may be quite speculative, so much so that his work is not meant *by him* to provide experimental information to normative politics; nonetheless, I think there is in every moral science, taking its light from practical principles, an *essential intention* to return to practice. On this hypothesis, sociology *in itself* will be an annex of normative political science, without thereby preventing the sociologist from excluding from his preoccupations the design of contributing to the direction of human conduct.

It is, in the strictest sense of the term, a physical science. By contrast, both economics and history, as well as sociology, may be considered moral sciences in the proper sense of the term, precisely because they depend for their explanations on activities of free agents in relation to ends appropriate to such agents. At the same time, however, we must not let pass unchallenged the persistent attempts to extend the scope of psychology to problems that are really problems of ethics and can only be understood in the light of moral principles. In fact, such efforts to subject all affective life to empirical speculative procedures of modern psychology go back at least three-quarters of a century. For instance, writing in the 1860s, a well-known author insisted that for psychology there are no good or bad passions any more than there are useful and harmful plants for the botanist. Such distinctions, he said, are what moralists and gardeners are interested in.[9] That is a seductive but sophistic parallel. To a plant it matters not whether it causes joy or its opposite in the lover of gardens; but a passion, considered in its concrete exercise, directly affects the moral destiny of the free agent. And that is why, when it studies human passions, psychology becomes less of a natural science than when it studies, say, memory. It may not be easy to draw a straight line between a psychological and an ethical problem, but it is safe to say that the moment the possibility of free choice enters the picture, psychology, if it eschews all value judgments, cannot provide a full explanation of the case.[10]

---

[9] Théodule Ribot, *English Psychology* (New York: D. Appleton and Company, 1874), p. 27.
[10] Ibid.

Leaving choice out of consideration cannot but distort our understanding of human experience, including emotional responses. We find in such attempts the last word of scientism.[11] After its arrogant pretension to subject metaphysical problems to the judgment of positive science, scientism is now working on the *physication of moral things*, so to speak. And what is particularly disturbing is that so many well-meaning people seem ready to concede to it so much of the contested ground, These people fuss about particular methodologies employed in contemporary social sciences, but they do not seem to object to their

---

[11] To avoid all equivocation, let us note that we do not share the opinion, which has spread even to certain laboratory psychologists, that a scientific or positive psychology entirely distinct from philosophical psychology would be possible. We believe in the possibility—already doubtless in large part realized—of an empiriological and empiriometric science of the things of the soul as distinct from philosophical psychology as chemistry is from cosmology. With two reservations, however: (1) Every time the psychologist, whether philosophical or experimental, confronts the concrete play of freedom, a reality whose intelligibility varies according to the moral value that it implies, he must necessarily have recourse to the practical light of moral science and, as there exists no empiriological ethics, the experimental scientist will in these matters be obliged to go to school to the philosopher, or even to the theologian (see below). (2) When the psychologist, whether philosophical or experimental, studies the facts of the religious life, recourse to the light of theology is absolutely required.

That does not mean that every study of the *concrete play of freedom* or of the religious life must be excluded from a book entitled *Treatise on Psychology*. Even with respect to such objects there is a way of treating questions that is proper to the psychologist and distinguished from that of the moral philosopher and the theologian. All we mean is that in these matters psychology, speculative science (whether philosophical or empiriological), is not sufficient unto itself.

classification as positive and speculative rather than moral and practical sciences. And that is why we must insist that no science of human action, of moral being, if it is to grasp its real object, can dispense with the knowledge of values received from moral philosophy.[12]

28. Actually, there is more to it. As we have seen,

---

[12] One can at least say that this undertaking has never encountered as little resistance as in our times, for the tendency is an old one. The social-political literature of the first half of the nineteenth century pullulates with claims—still having the bloom of youth—in favor of the recognition of a science of societies as rigorous, exact, and infallible in its applications as physics, chemistry, and mathematics. The unanimity is touching: traditionalists, liberal economists, positivists, socialists (utopian or "scientific") speak the same language. The prestige of Newtonian science turned the most genial heads. Do not be mistaken about the nature of these claims. It is not simply a question of taking knowledge of societies to that level of perfection that only the employment of the scientific spirit in research and reasoning can bring it—nothing could be more admirable. And there are some common qualities of the scientific spirit that have application, all differences being observed, whatever the object under consideration. Rather, it is a question of conferring on the science of the world of morality a rigor *univocally* like that which reigns in natural science, and this calls for conceiving the moral object after the manner of a physical object.

Note, too, in order to prevent dangerous illusions, that social physicalism is a conception much broader than social materialism and that one does not avoid the former because one avoids the latter. All declarations on the insufficiency of materialist explanations, the keenest concern to allow lots of room for psychic and spiritual factors, will not suffice, most of the time, to re-establish the understanding of morality, It is not only the mind that has to be recovered, but liberty. With respect to *moral being*, qualified by freedom, many things of the mind, being indifferent to human action in their specifications, still present the character of natural things. (That is why psychology, except when it bears on the conthe practical science that ought to rule the action of human beings destined to a supernatural end is not philosophy but theology. It is also theology that makes us understand the moral life actually lived by humanity, actually lived by a humanity born in Paradise, fallen through sin, redeemed by the sacrifice of God made man, worked on by grace and the devil, shuddered with miracles, and preceding on its way by the torches of prophecies. The intelligibility of the Hundred Years' War is not the same for one who believes and one who does not believe in the authenticity of the voices of Joan of Arc. The historical act of the *Syllabus* has not the same historical sense for one who sees it as a condemnation of dangerous errors and one who sees it as a condemnation of the most precious achievements of modern civilization.[13]

Must the Christian, then, sometimes withhold full agreement with the nonbeliever not only on the rules of conduct but also on the understanding of moral facts? This hard conclusion seems to follow.

---

crete life of liberty, remains a *physical science*—philosophical or empiriological.) In the notion of physicalism as we use it here, 'physical' should be understood *as opposed to* 'moral,' not as opposed to 'psychic'.

[13] Peter Wust, *Crisis in the West*, trans. E. I. Watkin, Essays in Order 2 (London: Sheed & Ward, 1931), p. 8: "We are to-day, one and all, too apt to forget the fact that history, in its deepest sense, does not consist merely of secular happenings, but that it is always at the same time a sacred process, a spiritual happening."

10

The Notion of Political Science: A Program

29. By repeatedly using examples from political science to exhibit the noetic characteristics and methods of moral philosophy, we have assumed in the preceding a position that is more controversial today than ever. Is politics a part of moral philosophy, or does it constitute an independent discipline? In the Aristotelian tradition, moral philosophy broadly conceived embraces not only the science of personal conduct but also the science of governing the household and the science of governing the city. But attractive as it is, this conception nevertheless involves a number of difficulties. And so we face the following problem: Either we must clarify its obscurities, or we must settle for a narrower notion of moral philosophy that excludes both economics and politics. It would, of course, be infinitely desirable to settle the problem of the practical sciences and their interrelations in its entirety. But this would require another complete treatise and thus lies beyond the scope of this work. More modestly, we hope simply to indicate here, with all the reserve that the extreme difficulty of the subject demands, no more than the basic conditions an inquiry into the relations of ethics and politics would seem to have to satisfy in order to have any chance of succeeding.

30. If our views are well founded, then, it would be necessary first of all to emphasize that practical thought is not fully intelligible at any stage except in relation to the *ultimate* practical judgment toward which it is directed from the beginning.

To think about any point on the road that goes from Athens to Thebes, it helps to know where Thebes is in relation to Athens. By analogy, to understand what the science of morality is one must know what prudence is. Likewise the theory of political science presupposes that one know the function of the statesman.

31. Confronting the term of practical discourse, the decisive question to ask is this: Are we dealing with a judgment of prudence or a judgment of art? The answer will determine if the practical science in question is one in the precise sense in which *praxis* is opposed to *poiesis*, or if it is a practical science only in a broad sense, as one calls practical the sciences that would be more accurately designated by the Aristotelian expression *poietic sciences*. Although Aristotle sometimes calls them both practical, art is not at all the same thing as prudence, and a science related to prudence is not at all the same thing as a science regulative of an art.

There is no doubt that here we touch on the most important and most difficult aspect of this entire problem. Is the specific intellectual quality required of the statesman an art or a virtue? Is what the statesman needs to perform his function satisfactorily something like what the architect, the gardener, or the cook needs to do his job well? Note that if that were so, statesmanship would be an intellectual quality one could fully possess even in the absence of moral virtues and good will. But can an intelligent rascal really govern a state just as perfectly as a cook who is a rascal can prepare an excellent meal? Or is it not, rather, that the specific quality required of the statesman intrinsically depends on the moral perfection of his will? Can one be a good chief of state without being first of all a good man?

32. To answer these questions, recourse to experience will not suffice. Among the rulers history counts as benefactors of their peoples, one finds all kinds of characters. Alongside some very honest and saintly personages, one sees others who were debauched and mean. But this in no way proves that a debauched person or a thief can be a good chief of state. In fact, even if we grant them a correct conception of the public good, historians are clearly attracted by the most visible events and tend to overlook intimate experiences. Thus, there will always be room to ask if some glaring benefit by reason of which a prince is adjudged great is not balanced by an invisible harm, or if some glaring reversal by reason of which a prince is judged mediocre is not balanced by a hidden benefit. Besides, accidental causality plays too great a role in political affairs for us to conclude from happy events that they were brought about chiefly by the ruler in charge. It sometimes happens that a state prospers under a ruler unworthy to be called a statesman, just as it happens that someone attains a great age despite excessive consumption of alcohol. Thus, it is not history that can tell us whether it is essential for a good chief of state to be a good man, or whether political wisdom is a prudence or only an art. The answer can be found only in a rigorous rational analysis of the concept of *political government.*

Political government is defined by its object, which all agree is the common good. The problem, therefore, comes down to knowing the order to which the common good belongs. If it belongs to the order of human action, the wisdom of the statesman is a prudence and political science is a part of moral philosophy. But if the common good belongs to the order of production, or making, political wisdom is an art, and political science, like architecture or agronomy, is intrinsically independent of moral philosophy. We think the alternative is absolute, and that it is impossible to conceive coherently political science as at once formally distinct from and intrinsically dependent on ethics.

33.   The answer clearly depends on our understanding of the common good and, above all, of moral good. Now, as long as we consider only personal conduct, the order of action is distinguished from the order of making with relative ease. True, the notions themselves of these two orders may not be completely free from obscurity even at this level, but there is little chance here of confusing the one with the other. But as soon as we go beyond problems of personal life, things tend to get confused, and the only way to keep them straight is to go to a *metaphysics of morality*. Here is, in outline, what needs to be done.

In the first place one might point out that in the order of moral finalities, as opposed to what obtains in the order of natural finalities, nothing is intelligible save in relation to the ultimate end of all things, the transcendent and absolute good—in a word, God. The good or bad functioning of the liver or pancreas, or of a railroad or a mill, can be described without taking into consideration anything but finite being. But it is impossible to define the moral quality of the will without relating it to the absolute Being whose nature will be correctly designated only if one recognizes in it the ontological unlimited or the Being that is identical to the plenitude of Being.[1] Thus, in order for a human being to dwell, so to speak, in the world of morality, simple knowledge of rules and desire for the good are not enough: what is required is the recognition that the rational faculty is open to the infinite and capable of God. The multiplicity of intermediary finalities is of little account here. For it is the relation to the absolute good that sustains liberty, regardless of all conceivable intermediaries between the immediate object of free choice and the ultimate end of the universe. Without this relation to the ultimate end, there can be no moral good or evil and thus also neither moral being nor liberty; wherever this relation intervenes to qualify freedom, we are in the presence of a moral being.

In the second place, one might point out that in its clearest realization moral being or moral quality is what is most interior to the soul, what touches most intimately the center of the personality. Although there is, abstractly speaking, more interiority in knowledge than in desire—for knowledge introduces into the soul an object which becomes its perfection, whereas desire draws the soul toward a perfection existing outside it—moral qualities are more interior to the soul than is knowledge itself, because in the moral

---

[1] For morality to exist, it is not necessary that the free act be explicitly related to God. It suffices that it be related to the absolute good whose personal reality and true name may be unknown or mistaken.

act the active causality of the soul plays a more considerable role than in knowledge. It is only as nature that the soul is the efficient cause of the qualities that knowledge confers on it. But when it comes to moral qualities, the soul acts as efficient cause twice: first as nature, second as liberty.

Note also that of all the realities that pertain to the order of morality, the first, both in itself and in our knowledge, has the character of a *terminal* act or of an action. One seeks conditions of life favorable to virtue only in order to acquire virtue, and one acquires virtue only in order to act virtuously. Thus, the *archetypical realization of the notion of moral being is the terminal act by which free will chooses for itself a definite relation to its ultimate end.*

34. Having thus clarified the notion of moral being and identified its most typical realization, let us ask now if the common good pursued by human society exhibits the requisite metaphysical characteristics of moral good. Is it a sort of good that requires reference to human liberty? Does the idea of the ultimate end necessarily enter into its definition? To answer these questions, we first turn to experience, which provides us with a sign of capital importance. While an engineer can say all he has to say about the construction of a bridge without revealing his religion, one can usually tell a man's religion from the ideas he has on the functions of the city. A metaphysics of man's ultimate end is implied by every political concept. No doubt, the same idea of the ultimate end is compatible with different opinions on how the city should be organized. The nationalistic state can be served by revolutionary fascism or conservative monarchism as God can be served in a republic or monar-

chy. But, true or false, the idea of the ultimate end is always there and commands, if not the detail of the means, at least the animating intention of the whole system. Whence also the incoherence of liberalism and its practical contradictions. Liberalism maintains that questions of ultimate human destiny belong exclusively to personal conscience and ought not in any way to enter into the structure and functioning of the city. But that said, liberalism immediately proceeds to set up a city whose organization and functions all clearly imply a determinate answer to the problem of human destiny. Thus, as soon as one ceases to think of liberty as liberals understand it, that is, as the supreme good of man as an individual, one's virtue becomes quite suspicious in the liberal state.

Indeed, the necessity of taking sides willy-nilly on the question of the ultimate end is so constant in politics that it cannot be considered a contingent matter; its roots lie in the nature of things. A specifically human product, born of intelligence, of liberty, and of virtue, society irresistibly tends to what in the order of finality is specifically human in us. For it is not just our material needs that bring us together in society. The anguish of the solitary man expressed in Sully-Prudhomme's famous sonnet would be even greater if those whose services he no longer enjoys were scientist, historian, and poet rather than laborer, weaver, and mason.[2] No more dreadful fate is imaginable than one in which the soul would have to hu-

---

[2] "Un Songe," in *Oeuvres de Sully Prudhomme. II. Poésies, 1866–1872* (Paris: Alphonse Lemerre, 1926), p. 51:

I dreamt the worker told me I must make my bread:
"I will no longer feed you; plow the earth and sow."
"Now you must make your clothes," the tailor said,

manize itself by itself. Our souls need company as much as our bodies, and that is why society, precisely as aiming at the properly human good of the human group in its earthly life, cannot ignore the relation of that good to the ultimate end of man. And the conclusion to which all this leads is not only that the common good pursued by society is indeed a moral good, but also that the quality required by the political man is not art but prudence and that political science is definitely a practical science.

35. But doesn't this contradict what we have said of the interiority, the incommunicable nature, of moral quality? What qualifies me morally is my own immanent act, proceeding from the most intimate source of activity in my nature. No mayor or chief of state could ever give me my liberty, because if they could, it would no longer be my liberty, and I would no longer have specific moral identity. Recall how St. Thomas opposes the *agibile interius* to the *factibile exterius*. Where there is no longer absolute immanence, doing is replaced by making, he says, and prudence by art.

We answer that this absolute interiority or immanence belongs only to the ultimate practical judg-

---

And masons told me, "You will grasp the trowel just so."
I was alone, abandoned by the human race
That everywhere I lagged behind, a pitiless curse
from heaven to which in hope of mercy I had turned
and on my path a pride of lurking lions burned.

Opening my eyes, I doubted the dawn I saw was real:
Goodly comrades whistled, their shoulders to the wheel,
Every trade at work and fields all full of seed.

Happiness I saw is in this world of ours
Where none should boast to best his neighbors
And ever since that day I've loved them all indeed.

ment and the act informed by it, which are the most typical and most readily intelligible realizations of the moral being. The terminal act of free will can proceed only from the will, which is in turn specified by it, and this *agibile* par excellence is necessarily and to the highest degree interior. But it does not follow at all that, because we stress the existential uniqueness of the most typical realizations of moral being, lest we misunderstand the nature of the whole system, morality simply disappears in the absence of total interiority. For *the system of moral being covers not only the immanent liberty of the terminal act of good or bad choice but also everything else that relates this act to the absolute good.*

Consider a mountain village whose inhabitants, because of difficulties in exchange, suffer from a misery and ignorance that make virtue practically impossible. In a case like this, it is the duty of the state to promote conditions that would help those people improve not only their material but also their spiritual situation. By itself, such intervention by the state cannot of course produce *virtue* in the souls of the inhabitants. But that does not mean that it cannot produce a complex of conditions favorable to spiritual development, and still less that the intervention is not in the final account aimed at moral good. We must never forget that the human conditions of morality, however exterior they may be or seem to be, still belong to the order of moral being. After all, not only are they defined with respect to the moral good; they are also willed because of it and by this relation of finality are safely linked up with its interiority.

36. If, then, we recognize that the moral good includes the common good of societies, at the same

time as we distinguish the good of a person, the good of the family, and the good of the city, it follows that we must also distinguish several sorts of prudence and, correlatively, several types of moral science. Thus, besides personal prudence, we should define a familial prudence, having for its object the common good of the domestic society, and a political prudence, having for its object the common good of the city; and, besides personal ethics, also an economic science and a political science. While this we cannot do here, we want at least to consider the question of priority of these diverse prudences and sciences within the total order of practical thought.

Two perspectives are readily identified. In a certain sense and under certain conditions (whose precise determination would be the object of a most useful but also most difficult study), the common good of the multitude appears preferable to the good of the individual, and one should not reject out of hand the Aristotelian notion of a subordination of ethics to politics. But, from another point of view, it seems that the primacy belongs to the good of an individual person, not only because the individual needs to attain his supra-temporal end, but also because even in the order of temporal ends it constitutes the moral good par excellence and lends intelligibility to the whole system of morality. We hold these two views not to be necessarily contradictory. For even if we grant that the most intelligible realization of moral goodness is found not in the common good but in the good man, the only conclusion we are led to is that it is the good man who determines the limits within which ends pursued in common must be kept lest they lose the character of moral good.

This is why to ask whether political science—and the same could be said of economics—is an autonomous science or subject to ethics is to ask the wrong question. In fact, such a juxtaposition shows a basic misunderstanding of the essentially and intrinsically moral character of the end pursued by politics. For moral regulation of politics would be heteronomic only if politics were essentially designed with a view to a good other than moral good. But since its object, the common good, is intrinsically moral, moral regulation of politics is all its own. And thus it is that those who, in opposing economic and political amoralism, speak of the need to submit economics and politics to ethics show only that they have not fully understood the irreducibly moral character of economics and politics.

We, therefore, also conclude that any conflict between the prescriptions of personal ethics and those of politics can be only apparent. These appearances, of course, will sometimes be violent and agonizing cases of conscience. But if the common good aimed at by politics is essentially an intermediary end related to man's ultimate end, it is impossible that any insoluble contradiction with the demands of the moral good of the person could arise. Moral good cannot be in contradiction with moral good, because the ultimate end in relation to which whatever is morally good is morally good cannot make contradictory demands. Were a city confronted with a choice between apostasy and the extermination of all its members, politics itself would prescribe the choice of extermination.³ The common good of the city, which by definition entails the virtuous life of the multitude as such, by that same fact entails indirectly but essentially respect for the vocation of its members to eternal life. That is why choosing, even at the price of the ultimate sacrifice, the way of salvation remains fully within the limits outside of which the common good of the city would lose its ultimate justification.⁴

37. One could stop there if man were destined only for a natural final end. No doubt, in the state of pure nature there would have been only one perfect society, the state, and political science would have been sufficiently defined as the practical science that looks to the common good of *the city*. But the assigning of a supernatural destiny to man gives rise to the institution of a spiritual city, in such wise that a complete theory of political science will require a particular elucidation of the notion of temporal good, guarding against conceiving it as a completely physical and material good, by too facile an assimilation to the spiritual and the moral.

38. But even after the idea of the temporal common good is thus clarified with regard to its moral and spiritual aspects, one question remains to be con-

---

³ See Guy de Broglie, S.J., "Science politique et doctrine chrétienne," in *Recherches de science religieuse*, 14 (March–April 1932), 145.

⁴ Eternal salvation is not the *direct* end of political society, whose end, although *moral*, is temporal. But, because the temporal common good is a moral good, it is essentially *related* to the eternal good, so much so that it would lose its nature and cease being a good if it ceased being related to the eternal good. It should not be inferred that the temporal common good is a pure means, a mere *utility*: neither pure means nor ultimate end, it is truly an end but essentially subordinate to an ulterior end.

sidered. Can we as Christians envisage a political science that, in its strictly scientific character, is independent from Christian theology? If it is true that even the temporal common good is a moral good, the principles established in the foregoing clearly require us to recognize that a Christian political science cannot be developed without appeal to the light of theology. Nevertheless, the exact relation between Christian theology and political science may be reasonably interpreted in two ways. Our knowledge of politics can be seen as a kind of political theology, a mere chapter of an infinitely higher discipline which admits of no division into distinct species. But, as Jacques Maritain has recently suggested, it is also possible to conceive a Christian political science that remains essentially philosophical and distinct from theology even while relying on its light.[5]

On the first view, the Christian political scientist would be no more than a specialized theologian, who could not do his job if he did not qualify purely and simply as a theologian. But, on the second view, while Christian politics would of course still require full adherence to the truths established by Christian theology, its practices would largely depend on the virtue of prudence and would not specifically require the presence of the theological *habitus*. We think that debating these two views is worthwhile. But whichever of them may prevail, what remains above any dispute is that the ultimate judgment upon politics belongs to theology.

---

[5] *Essay on Christian Philosophy.*

BIBLIOGRAPHY

Aquinas, Thomas. *Commentary on Aristotle's Nichomachean Ethics*. Trans. C. I. Litzinger, O.P. South Bend, Indiana: Dumb Ox Books, 1993.
Aristotle. *De anima*. Trans. J. A. Smith. In *The Works of Aristotle* III. Ed. W. D. Ross. Oxford: Clarendon, 1931.
―――. *The Nichomachean Ethics*. Trans. David Ross. Rev. J. L. Ackrill and J. O. Urmson. Oxford: Oxford University Press, 1925.
Baudin, Émile. *Introduction générale à la philosophie*. Paris: J. Gigord, 1921.
Bergson, Henri. *L'intuition philosophique*. Paris: Armand Colin, 1911.
Boutroux, Pierre. *Les mathématiques*. Paris: Albin Michel, 1922.
Brentano, Franz. *The Origin of Our Knowledge of Right and Wrong*. Trans. Roderick M. Chisholm and Elizabeth H. Schneewind. Ed. Roderick M. Chisholm. New York: Humanities Press, 1969.
Broglie, Guy de, S.J. "Reponse à une attaque," *Recherches de science religieuse*, 14 (March–April 1932), 135–50.
Buytendijk, F. J. J. *Vues sur la psychologie animale*. Cahiers de philosophie de la nature 4. Paris: J. Vrin, 1930.
Clairvoyance de Rome. Paris: Spes, 1929.
Comment juger la sociologie contemporaine. Entretiens de Juilly 3. Marseilles: Publiroc, 1930.

Garrigou-Lagrange, Réginald, O.P. *Le réalisme du principe de finalité*. Paris: Desclée De Brouwer, 1932.

Gilson, Étienne. *The Spirit of Mediaeval Philosophy*. Trans. A. H. C. Downes. New York: Charles Scribner's Sons, 1940.

Goblot, Édmond. *Essai sur la classification des sciences*. Paris: F. Alcan, 1898.

Gredt, Joseph. *Elementa philosophiae aristotelico-thomisticae*. 2 vols. Fribourg: Herder, 1909.

Janet, Paul. *Histoire de la science politique*. Ed. Georges Picto. 3rd ed. 2 vols. Paris: F. Alcan, 1900.

John of St. Thomas. *Cursus theologicus*. Ed. Monks of Solesmes. 4 vols. Paris: Desclée, 1931–1953.

———. *Cursus theologicus in Summam theologicam d. Thomae*. 10 vols. Paris: L. Vivès, 1883–1886.

———. *Logica*. Vol. 1 of *Cursus philosophicus thomisticus*. Ed. Beatus Reiser. 3 vols. Turin: Marietti, 1933.

Maritain, Jacques. *Art and Scholasticism*. Trans. Joseph W. Evans. New York: Charles Scribner's Sons, 1962.

———. *The Degrees of Knowledge*. Trans. Gerald B. Phelan. New York: Charles Scribner's Sons, 1959. Repr. Notre Dame, Indiana: University of Notre Dame Press, 1995.

———. *An Essay on Christian Philosophy*. Trans. Edward H. Flannery. New York: Philosophical Library, 1955.

———. *Réflexions sur l'intelligence et sur sa vie propre*. Paris: Nouvelle Librairie Nationale, 1924.

Maurras, Charles. *La musique intérieure*. Paris: B. Grasset, 1925.

Piéron, Henri. *Psychologie experimentale*. Paris: Armand Colin, 1934.

Rodier, Georges. *Aristote: Traité de l'âme.* 2 vols. Paris: Ernest Leroux, 1900.

Ribot, Théodule. *English Psychology.* New York: D. Appleton and Company, 1874.

Scheler, Max. *The Nature of Sympathy.* Trans. Peter Heath. Ed. Werner Stark. New Haven, Connecticut: Yale University Press, 1954.

Simon, Yves R., John J. Glanville, and G. Donald Hollenhorst. *The Material Logic of John of St. Thomas.* Chicago: The University of Chicago Press, 1955.

Sully Prudhomme. *Oeuvres de Sully Prudhomme. II. Poésies, 1866–1872.* Paris: Alphonse Lemerre, 1926.

Thomas Aquinas: Selected Writings. Ed. Ralph McInerny. Harmondsworth and New York: Penguin, 1998.

Viénot, Pierre. *Is Germany Finished?* New York: Macmillan, 1932.

Warren, Howard C. *Précis de psychologie.* Paris: M. Rivière, 1923.

Wust, Peter. *Crisis in the West.* Trans. E. I. Watkin. Essays in Order 2. London: Sheed & Ward, 1931.

INDEX

absolute good, 79
absolute Being, 79
absolute certitude, 20*n*
abstraction, degrees of, 31–34; two kinds of, 69
accidental causality, 77
Ackrill, J. L., xiii*n*
actual existence, 32, 33, 34, 36
affective connaturality, 17*n*, 19, 21*n*, 23, 41
affective knowledge, 17, 19, 20*n*
agibile, 83
agibile interius, 82
Albert the Great, 1*n*
Alphonsus Ligouri, St., 36, 42
America, 64
amor transit in conditionem objecti, 18*n*
amoralism, 85
analysis (*modo resolutorio*), 35, 45, 53
apparent good, 45
architect, 76
Aristotelian school, 42, 75
Aristotle, ix, xii, xiii, 1, 2, 5, 8*n*, 9*n*, 10, 13, 18*n*, 19*n*, 21, 25, 27, 31, 35, 36, 39, 43, 45, 46, 48. 58, 64*n*

art, xii, 9, 11, 15, 78
art/prudence, 82
Art and Scholasticism, 8*n*
asceticism, 60
Athens, 76
Augustinian, 54

Baudin, Émile, 5*n*
believer/nonbeliever, 74
Bergson, Henri, 22
Berkeley, 23
Bonaventure, St., xviii
bourgeoisie, European, 64
Boutroux, Pierre, 20*n*
Brentano, Franz, 10*n*
Buytendijk, F. J. J., 20*n*

Cajetan, vii, xi, xv, 5, 6, 7*n*, 12, 15*n*, 35*n*, 39, 70*n*
Catherine of Siena, St., 60
certitude of judgment, 15
Chisholm, Roderick, 10*n*
Christian political science, 87
Christian, 59, 74
Christian ethics, 59, 61
Christian morality, 68
Christian wisdom, 59
Clairvoyance de Rome, 58*n*, 68*n*
cogitativa, 35

common good, 61, 78, 83, 84, 86
commutative justice, 23
completely practical knowledge, xi, xii
concrete action, 49
contemplation, 53, 55
contingency, xiv
contingent, 9
contingent order, xvii
Cursus philosophicus thomisticus, 4n
Cursus theologicus, 5, 8n, 9n, 14n, 28n, 32n, 35n

de Broglie, Guy, 86n
De generatione et corruptione, 36
De progressu animalium, 36
De coelo et mundo, 36
decision, 38n
Deely, John, xvii
Degrees of Knowledge, The, 21n, 41n, 51n, 54n
deliberation, 38n
Delos, J.-T., 66n
Dionysian hierarchy, 29
directing action, 47, 53

earthly life, 82
economics, 71
efficient causality, 80
empiriological and empiriometric, 72n
end/desire, 47
end/means, 27, 63
Essay on Christian Philosophy, 61n, 87
essence, 34, 36, 48

eternal life, 86
ethics subordinate to politics, 84, 85
Evans, Joseph W., 8n
existence, abstracting from, 32
existential uniqueness, 83
experience, 64
experimental knowledge, 33n
extra genus notitiae, ix

factibile exterius, 82
faith, 59
fascism/monarchism, 80
final causality, 3, 11, 27, 48
first unmoved mover, 27
first operation of mind, 3
formal cause, 3, 11, 13
free act, 79n
free will, 80
free will, terminal act of, 83
freedom, 64, 67, 72n

gambling, 38
Garrigou-Lagrange, Réginald, 13n, 48n
general principles, 49
Germany, 67
gifts of infused love, 54
Gilson, Étienne, 59
Glanville, John J., 44n
Goblot, Edmond, 34n
God, 53, 54, 78, 79n, 80
God's knowledge, 32
good, 47
good man, 84
Gredt, Joseph, 35n, 44

INDEX

habitus, 11, 22, 28*n*, 44, 87
Heath, Peter, 17*n*
historian, 77
history, 71
Hollenhorst, G. Donald, 44*n*
homosexuality, 68
human action, 40, 73
human destiny, 81
Hundred Years' War, 74

immanent act, 82
In Boëthii de Trinitate, 8*n*
inclination, 17
incommunicability of prudential judgment, 38*n*
intellect, 55
intellectual connaturality, 19
intellectual virtue, 11, 12
intelligence, human and angelic, 29
interiority, 79
intuition, 23
intuitive speculative knowledge, 33*n*
involuntary action, xvii

Jacques Maritain Center, vii, xii
Joan of Arc, St., 74
John of St. Thomas, vii, xviii, 4*n*, 8*n*, 13, 14*n*, 15*n*, 18*n*, 28*n*, 31*n*, 32*n*, 33*n*, 35*n*, 42, 43, 44, 45, 50
John of the Cross, St., 42, 50, 53, 54, 58
judgment, 3

judgment, scientific and prudential, 29
judgment of prudence, 17, 18
justice, 4

knowledge, natural/revealed, 59
knowledge, speculative or practical, 26

Lallement, Daniel, 68n
Liberalism, 81
liberal state, 81
liberty, 81, 82
logic, 34

man redeemed, 74
Maritain, Jacques, vii, 2, 8*n*, 17*n*, 20*n*, 41, 50, 53, 61*n*, 87
marriage, 69
mathematical abstraction, 40
mathematician, 23
mathematics, 32; absence of good in, 40
Maurras, Charles, 18–19, 58*n*
McInerny, Ralph, xv*n*
medicine, 66
metaphysical abstraction, 52
metaphysician, 23, 59
Metaphysics, 40*n*
metaphysics, 40, 47
metaphysics of morality, 78
minimally practical knowledge, xi
modo compositivo (synthesis), 35, 37

modo resolutorio (analysis), 35
Monte Carlo, 38
moral act, 53
moral conviction, 21
moral finalities, 78
moral good, 78
moral philosopher, 52
moral philosopher/moral theologian, 72*n*
moral philosophy, 23, 40, 43, 47, 50, 73, 75
moral philosophy/theology, 58
moral principles, 71
moral science, 39, 84; as abstract, 37; sacred/profane, 63
moral sense (synderesis), 27, 28, 29, 30, 31, 41, 42, 48, 49, 58, 56
moral sense, first judgment of, 39; judgment of, 46
moral virtues, 77
moralist, 23
morality, 79
mystical experience, 53

natural inclination, 21
Newtonian science, 73*n*
Nicomachean Ethics, xiii*n*, 8*n*, 9*n*, 10*n*, 15*n*, 18*n*, 28*n*, 32*n*, 35*n*, 43, 45, 47*n*
noetic sphere, 51
normative judgments, 37

On the Soul, ix, 1, 25*n*
order of action/order of making, 78
original sin, 60

Parva naturalia, 36
person, 85
person, good of, has primacy, 84
personal autonomy, 38*n*
Peter of Auvergne, 1*n*
Phelan, Gerald B., 2*n*
philosopher-moralist, 39
philosophy of nature/empiriological science, 51, 55
Physics, 35, 36
Picot, Georges, 64*n*
Pieron, Henri, 52*n*
Plato, 12
poiesis, 76
political government, 77, 78
political life, 61
political science, 75ff.
politics and sociology, 65, 66, 67, 68
politics, normative, 65, 70*n*
possible extra-mental existence, 34
Posterior Analytics, 12*n*
practical discourse, 76
practical intellect, 2, 5, 7, 11
practical judgment, 15
practical knowledge, 1, 3, 4, 8; degrees of, viii, 6–7; two species of, 25
practical science, xi, 8, 38, 82
practical thought, universal/singular, 49
practical truth, 10, 12, 14, 47, 55, 56
practically practical knowledge, xiii

INDEX 97

practico-practical knowledge, 26
principles, 28n
principles, self-evident, 41
principles, supreme regulative, 40
Prohibition, 64
Protagoras, 19n
Proudhon, 23
prudence, three kinds of, 84
prudence, xi, xii, 9, 11, 56, 58, 76, 78, 82; a virtue of practical intellect, xiii
prudent man, 39, 56
prudential judgment, 14, 26, 28, 31, 37n, 46, 48, 56
psychologist, 52
psychology, 70, 73n
purely natural ethics, 60

Q. D. de veritate, 28n, 29n

rectified appetite, xvi
Reflexions sur l'intelligence, 17n, 20n
Reiser, Beatus, 31n, 33n
Rhetoric, 9n
Robot, Théodule, 71n
Rodier, Georges, 1n
Ross, W. D., ixn, xiiin, 1n
rules, 79

Scheler, Max, 17n, 20n
Schneewind, Elizabeth, 10n
scientism, 72
Scotus, 12, 15
self-evident practical principle, 28 n

Simon, Yves, vii–xix, 44n
Smith, J. A., ixn, 1n
sociological studies, 64
sociologist/moralist, 68, 70
sociology, 71
Socrates, 22
soul, 52, 53, 54, 79, 82, 83
speculative intellect, 11
speculative truth, 10, 28n
speculative/practical, 34
speculative-practical knowledge, 26
speculatively practical science, 50, 51
Spirit of Mediaeval Philosophy, The, 59n
spiritual development, 83
Stark, Werner, 17n
statesman, 76
statesmanship, art or virtue? 76, 77
suicide, 66
Sully-Prudhomme, 81–82
Summa contra gentiles, 8n
Summa theologiae, x, xv, 4, 8n, 9n, 11n, 14n, 58,
Summa theologiae, Ia, 14.16, x–xi, 6n, 17n, 28n
Summa theologiae, prima secundae, 43, 45
supernatural, 54
supernatural end, 74
supernatural order, 20n
supernatural virtue, 58
Syllabus, 74
syllogizing and moral philosophy, 63
synderesis (moral sense), 28n, 45, 49

98　INDEX

synthesis (*modo compositivo*), 35

Thebes, 76
Thinking, practical, three kinds of, x
Thomas Aquinas, St., ix, xv, 4, 6, 8n, 10n, 12n, 13, 14n, 15n, 21, 25, 28n, 36, 39, 41, 43, 45, 46, 50, 58, 64n, 69, 82
Thomas Aquinas: Selected Writings, xv
total concretion, 37n,
transcendent absolute good, 78
transcendentals, 40
truth and error, xvii
truth, practical viii, xv, xvi
truth, speculative, xv
truth, speculative/practical, 55, 56, 57

ultimate end, 27, 28, 31, 38, 78, 80, 82, 85

ultimate practical judgment, 76, 82
ultimate end, natural/supernatural, 60
Urmson, J. O., xiiin
ut in pluribus, xiv

value judgment, 65
values, human, 66
Vienot, Pierre, 67, 68n
virtually practical knowledge, xii
virtue, 18, 43, 83
virtues, psychology of, 44
virtuous circle, xvi, 16
virtuous man, 18, 24
virtuous will, 41

Warren, Howard C., 52n
Watkin, E. I., 74
way of negation, 22
will, 30, 31, 55
Wust, Peter, 74n

www.ingramcontent.com/pod-product-compliance
Lightning Source LLC
Chambersburg PA
CBHW072338300426
44109CB00042B/1726